What
Wives Wish
Their
Husbands
Knew
about Sex

What Wives Wish Their Husbands Knew about Sex

A GUIDE *for* CHRISTIAN MEN

RYAN HOWES, PhD, RICHARD RUPP, MFT
STEPHEN W. SIMPSON, PhD

BakerBooks
Grand Rapids, Michigan

Published by Baker Books
a division of Baker Publishing Group
P.O. Box 6287, Grand Rapids, MI 49516-6287
www.bakerbooks.com

Printed in the United States of America

Library of Congress Cataloging-in-Publication Data

Howes, Ryan, 1958–
    What wives wish their husbands knew about sex : a guide for Christian men / Ryan Howes, Richard Rupp, Stephen Simpson.
       p. cm.
    Includes bibliographical references.
    ISBN 10: 0-8010-6774-X (pbk.)
    ISBN 978-0-8010-6774-7 (pbk.)
    1. Sex role—Religious aspects—Christianity. 2. Sex—Religious aspects—Christianity. 3. Marriage—Religious aspects—Christianity. 4. Man-woman relationships—Religious aspects—Christianity. I. Rupp, Richard, 1972– II. Simpson, Stephen, 1969– III. Title.
BT708.H69 2007
248.8'425—dc22
                                    2006036895

None of the references in this book to clients or persons seen in counseling or psychotherapy are based on real people. No real names or other identifying information has been used. The "clients" mentioned are fictional characters representing a combination of traits and problems encountered by the authors in their work as psychotherapists. In cases where it was difficult to avoid revealing identifying information of a real person, the client gave permission for his or her story to be used in this book.

For Jennifer, Jhona, and Shelley

Contents

Introduction

It's Not Just What You Know . . .

Four women sit in a restaurant talking about their love lives. It could be a scene out of *Sex and the City* or any soap opera. Three of the women complain about their boyfriends, lamenting their shortcomings and dreaming of something better. The fourth woman, who has been sitting quietly with a smile on her face, speaks up and tells the others about her fiancé. He's a devoted Christian, she says, and the other women nearly drop their forks. "You are sooo lucky," says one. "How did you get a Christian man?" Then another woman says what the rest are thinking: "Everybody knows that Christian men are the greatest lovers in the world. I wish I had one."

A true story? If not, it should be. Two thousand years after the greatest Lover in history walked the earth, it's way past time that Christian men had such a reputation. If the hallmark of the Christian life is love, then Christian men should be renowned as the best lovers in the world. With Jesus as our example, along with the wisdom of the Bible on sex and love, Christian men have a unique advantage in knowing how to love. If you know Christ, then you already have the key to being a great lover. Knowing Christ frees a man to experience amazing love and incredible sex with his wife. The truth is, it's not just *what* you know about sex and love, it's *Who* you know.

So what happened? Although God intended Christian men to be the best lovers in the world, they don't have that reputation, and most never think of God having anything to do with sex. They don't know what their wives wish they knew—that being great in bed is part of being a great man. The only way to become a great lover is to become the man God intended you to become. After that, the rest is easy.

In our counseling practices, we see too many men in bondage to their sexuality. We see too many single men hiding their sexual nature under a bushel instead of letting it shine on a hill. They feel nothing but shame and regret about their God-given sexual desires. At the other extreme, we see men so consumed with lust that they don't know how to have a relationship with a woman, including a sexual one. Our goal is to set men free to love with passion and do it forever in marriage. The Bible says, "Where the Spirit of the Lord is, there is freedom" (2 Cor. 3:17). This freedom includes your sexuality. So why have Christian men experienced feelings of bondage and desperation in their sexual lives?

Most Christian men have a ball and chain locked around each ankle. One was slapped on by the Puritans and the other by the pornographers. The Puritan chain on your right ankle demands that male sexuality look more like the *asexuality* of angels—you shouldn't kiss a woman until your wedding, you shouldn't turn your head if a gorgeous woman walks by, and you shouldn't talk freely about sex with your wife. Tied up with all these shoulds and shouldn'ts, a man can feel like castrating himself, because the daily guilt is too much to bear.

The pornographers have an equally oppressive chain wrapped around your other leg. This chain also comes with some shoulds and shouldn'ts. You should only look at women as sex objects. You should never get tangled up in a committed relationship with a woman for the rest of your life. You should be totally uninhibited by shame or morality. And fidelity? That's for prudes and losers.

Puritanism and pornography have something in common. They make men cowards. Puritan sexuality makes a man about as passionate and assertive as a wet Chihuahua. Pornography encourages a man to avoid taking a risk on a real relationship. It makes a man terrified of being dependent or "trapped" in a relationship. He remains forever a boy and never a man.

It's time to break free and become the sexual man God created you to be. For Christian men, sex and love are meant to be partners. When you have one without the other, your marriage will be boring. We want this book to help you bring sex and love together. Great lovers see no separation between sex and love. But to become a great lover, you have to be free—free from the Puritans and pornographers, from legalism and recklessness, from repression and exhibitionism.

This book will explore three sources of wisdom intended to set you free and make you the world's greatest lover. First, we'll turn to the Word of God. Some things in the Bible—like poetry about oral sex (see Song of Songs 4:16–5:1)—might surprise you. In the Bible we find eroticism done right instead of the cheap imitations coughed up by the pornographic posers. This is our chance to reclaim eroticism and learn what is *really* sexy from the Creator of sex.

We'll also draw on scientific research and lessons we've learned from working with hundreds of men in therapy. We'll explore the myths that keep men in bondage and shame and offer biblical truths that can set you free to love anew. We will also discuss common sexual problems and offer practical solutions.

Lastly, we speak to you man to man. Proverbs 27:17 says that one man sharpens another like iron sharpens iron, so we speak to you not only as therapists but also as guys who are trying to love their wives. We examined our own sexual lives while writing this book, just as we hope you'll examine yours while reading it. We'll tell you about some of our mistakes and the things that helped us love our wives better. We want to be great lovers for our wives, trying to practice what we preach.

So what do women wish their men knew about sex? The reality is that women and men actually wish for the same thing. We both wish for intimacy, lifelong love, trust, respect, fun, and romance. We both want hot, mind-blowing sex. The only challenge is that we approach these wishes from different angles. With God in your heart and a little extra knowledge in your head, you'll be able to overcome this challenge and make your wife's wishes as well as your wishes come true. This is what we'll explore to make that happen:

1. *The naked truth about God and sex.* If you're going to experience the fullness of your sexuality and lovemaking with your wife, you must embrace God's joy over your sexuality and reject notions that it is inherently sinful.
2. *How to be a man.* Christian manhood starts with leaving boyhood, so we'll help you find the keys to drive off into yours. Great lovers have to be great men first, so we'll explore crucial elements of the masculine identity.
3. *How to love a woman.* Being a great lover means knowing how to make love to your wife with intensity, intimacy, and passion—in and out of the bedroom—for the rest of your life.

Paul wrote, "It is for freedom that Christ has set us free" (Gal. 5:1 NIV). The Lord has the keys to set you free from anything that binds your God-given sexuality. He meant you to be free: free from shame, free from sin, free from selfishness, free from ignorance and fear, free to be yourself, free to be one flesh, free to love every inch of your wife's body, and free to be the world's greatest lover.

This book will unlock the shackles the Puritans and the pornographers have put in your life. It's time that Christian men had a new reputation. As you practice the ideas of this book, your wife may be bragging about you in a restaurant someday. And as you become the sexual man that God created you to be, your wife will be getting even more than she could ever have wished for.

PART ONE

Knowing Truth

1

Knowing in the Biblical Sense

When I (SS) told my father I was working on a book about sex for Christian men, he said, "I didn't think Christians had sex." Dad was joking, of course. He's a devout Christian and knows better. (And, of course, if he wasn't joking, there are my two sisters and me to explain.) But his response was telling. It's the view much of the world has of Christianity. They think we're prudes. They think we're about as interested in sex as a lethargic koala bear. Though this is an unfair judgment, we've done a lot to perpetuate the myth.

In case you don't believe me, let's do an experiment. Try to recall the number of sermons, Sunday school lessons, or Bible studies you've heard about how sinful and dangerous sex is. You don't need an exact number, just ballpark it. My guess is you broke double digits.

Now try to remember the number of times you heard something about sex being good, and I don't mean permissible, such as, "It's okay once you're married." I mean someone told you that sex is a blast and God made it that way on purpose. You probably don't remember hearing that message as often as the warnings about sex, but you've likely heard about sex being good a handful of times.

Now let's go a step further. How often have you heard about sex being great *and* heard it supported by Scripture? If you had to use more than one hand to count the number of times you've heard about the good stuff the Bible has to say about sex, consider yourself lucky. We tend to give more airtime to the bad stuff. Usually we talk about premarital sex, adultery, lust, pornography, homosexuality, abortion, and the perils of kissing on the first date. We've cornered the market on telling the world how much trouble sex can cause.

It's important to encourage sexual purity, especially when so much in popular culture promotes lust. However, relaying this message hasn't been our problem. We're good at that. When I was a youth pastor fresh out of college, I was especially good at it. I had the kids convinced that they would spontaneously combust at the first impure thought, but I failed to give them the full picture. I didn't tell them that sex is great, God made it that way, and being a Christian means you can have the hottest, most exciting sex in the world.

Why do I believe that? Because of the Bible.

A Balanced View of Sex

It's probably not correct to say we'll provide a "balanced" view of sex from the Bible. We're going to talk about positive views of sex that are in the Bible. There is plenty of stuff in Scripture that talks about chastity, guarding against lust, and avoiding temptation. It's potent wisdom and it needs to be studied. However, we'll go out on a limb and assume that you're familiar with those verses. If you aren't, go on the Internet and do a search on the words *sex* and *Bible*.

Let's start at the beginning. Genesis 2:25 says, "And the man and his wife were both naked, and were not ashamed." Let that sink in—*naked and not ashamed.* Letting it all hang out and thinking nothing of it. Nowadays, if you're naked and unashamed too much, you'll end up in jail. Parents teach their kids early not to walk around in the buff, because few cultures condone it.

So how did we get so far from Adam and Eve running around naked with a clean conscience? You know the rest of the story. They defied God by eating the forbidden fruit and then "they knew that they were naked" (see Gen. 3:6–7). Their sin separated them from God, resulting in shame because of their nakedness.

The striking thing is that *nakedness was not shameful until Adam and Eve sinned*. Shame about nudity was not part of God's initial plan. It's a curse. God never meant sexuality to be embarrassing. Adam and Eve's sin wasn't being naked; it was disobedience. It was selfishness. Embarrassment about sexuality resulted from sin, rather than sexuality itself being a sin.

Now we're not advocating some sort of Christian nudist position. By all means, keep your clothes on in public. However, the creation story lets us know that sexuality in its original state was good. Your sexuality is not a curse; it's a gift, and only sin corrupts it.

The Old Testament Hebrews knew this. They gave the sexual relationship between a man and wife high priority. A newly married man was given a year off from work to stay home and "be happy with the wife whom he has married" (Deut. 24:5). How different that is from modern culture! We give new couples a one-week honeymoon, as if it's a big reward for two or three decades of abstinence. The ancient Hebrews provided community support for a whole year so the couple could spend time with each other, build a relationship, and go wild in the bedroom.

Both Old and New Testament writers knew that a healthy sex life is crucial to a healthy marriage. Proverbs 5:18–20 doesn't mince words about an active marriage bed acting as a deterrent to adultery.

> Let your fountain be blessed
>   and rejoice in the wife of your youth,
>   a lovely deer, a graceful doe.

> May her breasts satisfy you at all times;
>   may you be intoxicated always by her love.
> Why should you be intoxicated, my son, by another woman
>   and embrace the bosom of an adulteress?

Paul was also clear that a husband is to love his wife (Eph. 5:25; Col. 3:19) and have sex with her regularly so he can avoid infidelity (1 Cor. 7:2–5).

Though these Scriptures make it plain that sex is an important part of marriage, there's a whole book of the Bible that makes sex sound downright glorious.

Eight Lessons from the Song of Songs

According to Jewish tradition, Solomon wrote three books paralleling the three stages in life—the Song of Songs for youth, Proverbs for maturity, and Ecclesiastes for old age. The Song of Songs, also known as the Song of Solomon, is an ode to the joy of sex. It's a series of erotic poems in the form of dialogue between a bride and groom. The title "Song of Songs" suggests that it is the greatest of all songs. Rabbi Akiba ben Joseph said, "Heaven forbid that any man in Israel ever disputed that the Song of Songs is holy. For the whole world is not worth the day on which the Song of Songs was given to Israel, for all the Writings are holy and the Song of Songs is the Holy of Holies" (Mishnah Yadayim 3:5). Theologian Dietrich Bonhoeffer said, "one could hardly have a more passionate and sensual love than here is portrayed. It is a good thing that that book is included in the Bible as a protest against those who believe that Christianity stands for the restraint of passion."[1] We have an entire book of the Bible devoted to love, passion, sex, and nothing else—nothing about unclean foods, idol worship, or various reasons to stone somebody. God isn't even mentioned. Theologian Michael Cosby says of the book, "Considerations of the best way to navigate the sea of life are ignored completely. Here there is only the pure enjoyment of playing in the water."[2] It's as if the Lord reserved this spot of the Bible for a poem of passion, in case anybody thinks that sex is only for the depraved.

The amazing thing is that I can't remember *ever* hearing a sermon about the Song of Songs. In fact, some Christians seem to have written off this part of the Bible. We don't know what to do with something so "naughty." This isn't true in certain Jewish traditions. Ashkenazic Jews chant the Song of Songs during Passover and many Sephardic Jews chant it on the eve of *every* Sabbath.[3] That's once a week. These rituals acknowledge the importance of the Song of Songs, an importance that Christians often miss.

When I was in junior high, my best friend and I used to read the Song of Songs during quiet time on youth choir trips. We cracked ourselves up trying to decipher what we thought were dirty metaphors. I wish someone had taken the time to explain that I wasn't reading biblical porn. I wish someone had shown me that the Song of Songs reveals powerful principles for experiencing passionate love with a woman.

Let's look at eight lessons the Song of Songs teaches us about passion, so we understand it as more than a potential giggle fest for bored teenagers.

Anticipation

The first lesson is that anticipation is the best part of passionate love. In the Song of Songs, the two lovers spend most of their time fantasizing about each other or searching for one another. The book has a tone of *anticipation*—there is little description of actual lovemaking. Most of the Song is about longing. "O that his left hand were under my head, and that his right hand embraced me!" says the woman in 2:6.

In 3:1–5 the woman searches the city for her groom. She asks other women and the city guards where he is. She becomes desperate. Then she finds him, and their reunion is sweet and passionate. But notice what she says in verse 5: "Do not stir up or awaken love until it is ready!" What? This woman has been running crazy around the city looking for this man, and then tells us not to awaken love until it is ready?

She tells us this because she knows that anticipation makes for really good sex. Women like the buildup. What they *don't* like is an abrupt invitation to lovemaking followed by two minutes of foreplay. Expectation, anticipation, and longing for the moment make sex more powerful. It's like building up a good appetite. Food tastes better when you're hungry. For a woman to thoroughly enjoy lovemaking, she needs to be hungry.

Now we don't believe the Song suggests that you send your wife on a wild-goose chase through town before the two of you make love. You shouldn't withhold or tease, but you should take the time to create an atmosphere of anticipation. There should be a sense of mystery and waiting. A phone call, a card, flowers, or affectionate words create a longing for physical intimacy. Sex shouldn't be something you squeeze in at the end of the day. It's something to cultivate throughout the day. And that makes for a great night.

The Value of the Pursuit

The second lesson is that the woman wants to be pursued.

When I was on the wrestling team in high school, I dreaded the first week of practice. Coach Griggs allowed anyone who survived the first week to be on the team. For five days he would reduce us to mush with physical conditioning. On the first day of practice there would be more than fifty guys coming out for the team. By the end of the week there would be about twenty. The only ones left were the guys passionate about wrestling, which is exactly what Coach wanted.

Women are a little bit like my wrestling coach (only more attractive). They need to see your desire and passion. I've heard all kinds of nasty names thrown around for women who play "hard to get," but why shouldn't they play hard to get? Why on earth would a woman enter an intimate relationship with a man who hasn't proved that he's serious about his desire for her?

In Song of Songs 7:10 the woman says, "I am my beloved's, and his desire is for me." There is a reason she knows this. The guy has worked hard to earn her passion. First, he praises her beauty. Second, he works hard to get her attention. "O my dove, in the clefts of the rock, in the covert of the cliff, let me see your face, let me hear your voice; for your voice is sweet, and your face is lovely," he says in 2:14. The woman he loves is hidden in the "clefts" of the rock, and he must call to her and praise her voice and face to get her to come out. In 4:12 he describes her as "a garden locked" and "a fountain sealed." He knows that she's not readily available for him whenever he feels like it. That's the reason we see the man in the Song of Songs constantly seeking his bride and praising her beauty.

Women like to be pursued. This is true whether you've been married forty minutes or forty years. Your wife wants to know that your desire is for her. She wants to feel special. It helps her to be free and vulnerable in the bedroom. It's hard to experience total, fulfilling intimacy if you aren't sure how someone feels about you. Even if you are sure, it helps if there are concrete expressions of those feelings. The man in the Song does this by inviting his beloved to dinner (2:4) and lavishing her with compliments. Thousands of years later, men still need to do the same.

The Need for Foreplay

Foreplay is essential. This is the third lesson. The guy in the Song of Songs is good. In today's parlance, "he's got game." He knows exactly what to say and how to impress his lady. Most of his lines are devoted to eloquent metaphors proclaiming his bride's beauty.

> Your eyes are doves behind your veil. Your hair is like a flock of goats, moving down the slopes of Gilead [she has beautiful long black hair] (4:1).

> Your lips are like a crimson thread, and your mouth is lovely (4:3).

> How graceful are your feet in sandals, O queenly maiden! Your rounded thighs are like jewels, the work of a master hand (7:1).

Now I wouldn't recommend quoting these verses to your wife word for word. These compliments were more endearing in the tenth century BC, when, most likely, the Song was written. However, the guy in the Song knows what he's doing. He knows that his bride wants to feel beautiful; she needs to know that her husband thinks she's hot.

Of course, physical beauty isn't the most important quality in a woman; her heart is. But if she's going to be vulnerable with you, if you're going to turn her on, she needs to feel gorgeous. A woman who doesn't feel this way may be more guarded during physical intimacy. The guy in the Song works hard to make his bride know that he has physical desire for her.

But foreplay isn't just about compliments. It's about creating a mood, an atmosphere that promotes lovemaking. Couples with a healthy sex life see foreplay as a lifestyle. The man in the Song of Songs understands this. "He brought me to the banqueting house, and his intention toward me was love," says the woman in 2:4. He's taking her to dinner! Some rituals never die. He's taking her out for a nice meal, and she knows exactly what his "intentions" are. He treats her to a romantic evening that makes her "faint with love" (v. 5), and she longs for his touch (v. 6). Here again she gives her admonition not to "stir up or awaken love until it is ready" (v. 7).

Don't expect to throw out a few compliments, take her to dinner, and then hop right in the sack. Remember, foreplay should be a constant. When you're doing the dishes, washing the car, or even taking care of the kids, these are opportunities for foreplay. For example, my idea of romancing my wife is flowers, a great dinner, and going to the theater or a concert. She enjoys those things, but you know what really turns her on? It's when I clean the house. It seems like the least romantic thing in the world to me, but she eats it up. It shows that her needs are important to me. This reminds me that foreplay is a process, a lifestyle. Just as the man in the Song is always seeking his beloved, so must we have a constant attitude of seeking our wife and making her feel loved.

The Joys of Physical Intimacy

Lesson four is physical intimacy should be part of reunion. The Song gives us several descriptions of lovers seeking each other, and guess what happens once they find each other? You know what happens.

Whether explicitly or through metaphor, the writer of the Song tells us that physical intimacy is part of reunion. He is subtle when he tells us that they go into the "garden" alone for a while (Song of Songs 4:16; 6:2) and not so subtle when he describes them going into the bed chamber (3:4). In the Song we observe cycles—the lovers are separated and come back together. Once they're together again, they're eager to make love.

Frequently in the modern world, husband and wife are separated. Each has responsibilities that drag the two away from each other. If you have kids, one of you is usually running around town managing the life of your children, while the other is at work. If you don't have kids, there's a good chance both of you are up to your neck with work, school, and/or church duties. When you're home, there's food to prepare, dishes to wash, and other domestic duties. How often is physical intimacy part of your reunion? And I don't mean a peck on the cheek or a hug. You know what I mean.

I had a client whose career was taking off and eating up a lot of his time and energy. He said that he was too tired or distracted to have sex when he got home. I asked him if he ever put lovemaking on his schedule, as he did so many other things, if he planned on seducing his wife. He said that he hadn't but that he would try it. The next day, from the moment he got out of bed, he decided that sex with his wife would be on his schedule. It was in the back of his mind all day. On his drive home, he started mentally preparing for it, just like he would a big event at work. By the time he got home, he was raring to go, and his wife was, shall we say, pleased. All it took was a slight attitude adjustment. Obviously the couple in the Song have sex on the brain much of the time. The same thing will work for you. Remember that great sex is more about a lifestyle and an attitude than what happens in the bedroom.

Pleasure and the Body

The body was made for pleasure. This is lesson five. One of the great heresies is that all desires of the flesh are sinful. If you believe that, just read the Song of Songs. Seriously, pick it up right now. It's only seven chapters, so it won't take long.

Finished? Good. Now answer this question: *If all desires of the flesh are sinful, what is this book doing in the Bible?* In it there are myriad images of physical pleasure. The bulk of this book describes how hot the couple is for each other and the physical excitement they derive from their union. There are far too many of these to list, but let's look at a few.

"Until the day breathes and the shadows flee, turn, my beloved, be like a gazelle or a young stag on the cleft mountains" (2:17). Why does she ask him to be like a stag on the "cleft mountains"? If we take this at face value, we might think she wants the guy to be leaping around on the edge of a cliff. But the Song is poetry, so it invites us to look deeper. She isn't asking for acrobatics; she wants him to fondle her breasts. The "cleft" is her cleavage and the "mountains" are her breasts. This woman obviously doesn't see the flesh as sinful.

"You are stately as a palm tree, and your breasts are like its clusters. I say I will climb the palm tree and lay hold of its branches. O may your breasts be like clusters of the vine, and the scent of your breath like apples, and your kisses like the best wine that goes down smoothly, gliding over lips and teeth" (7:7–9). The man is speaking here and, like most men, he's not as subtle as the woman was. He tells us what he really means by the "clusters" of the palm tree, and then tells us what he wants to do with them. Then he compares her kisses to wine. Things are getting downright decadent! Both the man and the woman talk about getting busy "until the day breathes and the shadows flee." They enjoy what they're doing enough to continue till morning.

The writer of the Song loves food references:

With great delight I sat in his shadow, and his fruit was sweet to my taste (2:3).

Let my beloved come to his garden, and eat its choicest fruits (4:16).

I come to my garden, my sister, my bride; I gather my myrrh with my spice, I eat my honeycomb with my honey, I drink my wine with my milk (5:1).

I went down to the nut orchard . . . to see whether the vines had budded (6:11).

I would give you spiced wine to drink, the juice of my pomegranates (8:2).

What is it with these two and food? Of course, there's a long tradition of sex and food going together, whether in foreplay or the act itself, but I think there's something more going on here. The author uses eating and food as sexual metaphors for a reason. The body is hardwired to respond to food with pleasure. Hunger alerts us to the fact that we need to eat. While eating, our response is pleasure. Whether it's the taste of the food or the satisfaction of filling our stomachs, the brain indicates that the body's needs are met by sending signals of delight and gratification. God could have done it another way. We could have felt pain as a signal that our stomachs are full (which happens when we overdo it). We could have started itching to indicate that our needs have been met. But God chose pleasure as the primary reward for nourishment. He did the same with sex. We have a need for physical contact and intimacy with our wife. God made a woman's body pleasing to us, and he made sex feel good so we would meet that need. When we regard all desires of the flesh as sinful, we reject God's plan and design. So when your wife's "vine has budded" in the "nut orchard," it's exactly what God had in mind.

Equality in Sex

Lesson six is man and wife are equal when it comes to sex. Nowhere in the Song does one member of the couple dominate the other. The woman is just as bold in her desire as the man. We never get the sense that one of them is in charge, especially in the bedroom. The structure of the Song suggests this by alternating stanzas between the man and the woman. (In many newer Bible versions, the speakers of the various stanzas are indicated.) Neither of them is calling all the shots.

In the bedroom men and women should play equal and similar roles. The woman may want to be pursued during foreplay, but there shouldn't be a pursuer or pursued in the bedroom. Husband and wife are both active participants when it's time to get it on.

I've worked with couples where the woman says something like, "I didn't know I was allowed to move during sex." The Song shows us that this shouldn't be the case. This woman knows that she can be engaged and active in the bedroom. We're not saying that a man and woman need always have the same level of arousal, but our wife needs to feel free to express her sexual wants and desires.

In Song of Songs 1:6–7 the woman's family detains her, forcing her to keep their vineyards to the neglect of her own, but love draws her away. A man's love should be freeing not restricting. If one of you feels controlled by the other, then your sex life, and probably the rest of your relationship, needs work. The bedroom is not a place for domination; it should be a place of freedom and vulnerability.

Retreat in Passion

Here is lesson seven: passion is the couple's retreat from the rest of the world. In Song of Songs 7:11–12 the woman takes the man out of the village, through the fields to the vineyards and says, "There I will give you my love." They are leaving the rest of the world behind to go make love.

The gardens and vineyards in the Song function not only as sexual metaphors but also as symbols of seclusion. They are a respite from the demands of the world. They show us that a man and woman need to retreat and be alone. If this was important when the Song was written, it is more so today. Never have there been so many things to distract a couple from each other. Demands on our time and energy swarm like locusts. If a couple doesn't find their own vineyard, those demands will devour intimacy.

Song of Songs 8:6–7 describes what the bond between a man and a woman should look like: "Set me as a seal upon your heart, as a seal upon your arm; for love is strong as death, passion fierce as the grave. Its flashes are flashes of fire, a raging flame. Many waters cannot quench love, neither can floods drown it. If one offered for love all the wealth of one's house, it would be utterly scorned."

The bond between a husband and wife should be a "seal." It should be "strong as death." The passion should be "a raging flame." Favoring wealth over love should be "scorned." This is the type of relationship a couple needs to withstand the distractions of the world. We should be fierce in our passion and devotion to our wife. We should scorn wealth and success if it threatens intimacy. When the locusts gather, you should escape with your wife to a secret garden, where the two of you can renew your connection and passion. Sometimes that will mean a vacation to a romantic locale. However, scheduling regular times of passion with your wife and creating your own special vineyard in your home will also protect your relationship. A hot and heavy hour or two in the bedroom will go a long way toward promoting and safeguarding intimacy. It's also a lot of fun.

The Foxes

Catch the little foxes is cryptic lesson eight. It comes at the end of chapter two: "Catch us the foxes, the little foxes, that ruin the vineyards—for our vineyards are in blossom" (Song of Songs 2:15).

Lillian Hellman derived the title of her play, *The Little Foxes*, from this verse. The play is about greed corrupting and destroying a family. Likewise, there are "little foxes" that can "ruin" the special vineyard that you and your wife create. As in Hellman's play, selfishness is one of the most dangerous foxes. Whenever one of you looks exclusively to your own needs, it will ruin intimacy. There are other things that can spoil your vineyard. Anger, fear, shame, resentment, apathy, poor communication, infidelity, pornography, and distraction are just a few that we'll examine in detail later in the book.

You must catch these little foxes. If you want a healthy sex life, you will have to watch for anything that can inhibit intimacy, both in and out of the bedroom. When you notice something creating distance or bad feelings between you and your wife, don't ignore it. Address it directly, without manipulation or malice. This is harder than it sounds. Notice that the foxes are "little." These aren't big wolves that dash in to eat you up. The Song doesn't warn us of the big problems—men, in particular, are good at handling those. It warns instead of the small, insidious evils that creep in slowly and unnoticed. Maybe it's hurt feelings that fester into resentment. Perhaps you've allowed a seed of lust for other women to grow and spread. Or maybe you've just let stress and distraction create distance between you and your wife. Whatever it is, you have to stop it. Whether through prayer, counseling, increased communication, or just a nice weekend away, keep those mangy little foxes out of your vineyard. In chapter 10, we'll talk about how to do this for life.

God's Template for Intimacy

Some regard the Song of Songs as a metaphor for God and the church. They believe the "lily of the valleys" and "the rose of Sharon" (v. 1) represent Christ, or that the man represents Christ and the woman represents the church. However, there's no evidence that the writer was talking about anything more than passion between a man and a woman. Most scholars agree that the Song is pure love poetry. The sexual tone of the Song is too strong for it to be otherwise. We doubt Christ would use some of the graphic descriptions in the Song to describe his feelings for the church. We believe this allegorical interpretation of the Song sprang from discomfort that such a sexual book is in the Bible. However, we accept it as a source of *comfort*. God didn't leave matters of sex to the porn industry or your seventh-grade health teacher. He gave us a whole book of the Bible devoted to the joy, mystery, and passion of sex.

Whenever we're asked to speak about sexual issues, the crowd usually wants to hear about the potential problems. They want to know about the prohibitions in the Bible and just how screwed up someone can become when they make the wrong decisions. We're happy to talk about that stuff because it's important, but the audience gets a bit of a shock when we start talking about the Song of Songs. They're surprised that God provided guidelines for what *to* do, rather than only what *not* to do. Thank God for the Song of Songs. In it he's given us a template for passion and intimacy, as well as some really sexy poetry.

A New (yet Old) Language for Sex

The Song gives us a terminology for talking about sex. Sex is supposed to be exciting and fun. When Christians talk about sex, it usually sounds neither. A lot of men go nuts at marriage enrichment retreats because all the language about sex is soft, lacy, and babyish. It sounds nothing like the sex we want to have.

This leaves Christian men with the technical terms—the biological terms, like coitus, penis, testicles, vagina, fellatio, cunnilingus, and ejaculation. None of these words are sexy. None of them are fun. These words make sex sound about as exciting as a trip to the urologist.

The other alternative is making sex sound superspiritual. While the best sex is always a spiritual experience, we sometimes describe it in ways that exclude the fun and erotic aspects. In church the words we've most often heard in reference to sex are *holy, powerful, union,* and *sacred.* While every one of these words is appropriate, they still don't adequately describe the sex most of us want to have. It sounds like part of a liturgy or a mystic ritual. Good stuff, but still nothing that makes you think of getting hot and heavy with your wife. The spirit is emphasized at the expense of our God-designed flesh.

And forget about being funny, lest you're accused of being disrespectful. It's a shame, because humor makes sex so much easier to talk
about, as long as it's not degrading. Christians might sound smart or
wise about sex once in a while, but we're almost never funny unless it's
by accident.

We don't have a good vocabulary for sex. Once again, the pornographers and Puritans spoiled it for us. The pornographers came up with
crass words for sexual acts and parts of the body. Though some of these
words are harmless, the pornographers claimed them for their own. The
Puritans followed up by slapping an "obscene" label on them. It's sad
because a few of these words aren't degrading at all. Some are even kind
of fun. But culture considers them profane, so most Christians never use
them unless they're out of earshot of anyone who would care. You and
your wife might have even spoken them on a night when things got a
little wild, but you wouldn't dare use them in the light of day.

Talking about sex is important for great lovers. First of all, you have to
talk to your wife about sex. It's important to communicate with her before
lovemaking even begins so you both understand each other's needs and
desires. You'll also want to talk to each other while making love, expressing your passion out loud, and telling one another what you like. During
such times, a word like *coitus* won't express the passion you feel. It might
even do the opposite. Your wife could break out in a fit of laughter, and
all plans for coitus might go out the window.

A great lover also talks with other men—his sons, brothers, and
friends—about sexuality. It's different, of course, than the conversation
he has with his wife, but he's not ashamed to discuss sex with other men.
When he does so, he probably doesn't want to use words like *penis* and
testicles. Just as he wants to use words that are sexy and fun with his
wife, he'll want to use words that are casual and even humorous with
other men.

Because of this, many men resort to "dirty" words. That might be okay
if a man avoids the degrading words, but it's still pretty lame. He has to

borrow words from the pornographers, and great lovers deserve better than that. But if he doesn't borrow from them, he's left with the medical terms that make sex sound technical and boring.

Late one night I pondered this problem while preparing a talk on sexuality for a group of seminary students. I wanted the talk to be direct and specific, but the last thing I wanted to do was stand in front of them using words like *testicles*. Of course, I wasn't going to use secular slang either, if I ever wanted to be invited back. I realized that Christians need their own language for sexuality, something new and exciting. I had no idea what to do.

When the solution hit me, I felt stupid that I hadn't realized it sooner. I'd known all along where the answer lay. My mistake was trying to think of something new, when what I really needed was something *old*. God gave us a vocabulary for sex long ago. It's been there for millennia, staring us in the face, waiting to be used. The fun, sexy vocabulary we need is in the Bible, in our old friend the Song of Songs.

Sexy talk was in the Bible long before the pornographers crafted the first four-letter word. In other words, *Christians* had a vocabulary for sex before the Puritans or pornographers started messing up the works. We have only to avail ourselves of these words. Below is a glossary of biblical images for sexuality. Use it with your wife to be sexy and fun, use it to have fun discussions with other men, and use it to make talking about sex a lot less awkward.

We didn't take liberties with Scripture to come up with these terms. Most of these references were common in erotic poetry during the period when the Song was written. Readers of the time would have gotten the double entendres. Though our exegetical work is solid, no one can be 100 percent sure what the author of the Song intended. In rare instances, we made educated guesses guided by research.

This glossary isn't exhaustive. We encourage you to read the Song of Songs and pick out some of your own fun and sexy terms. Even if your interpretations aren't 100 percent accurate, the words you pick will still be better than the crude attempts of the pornographers or biological terms from sex ed. We hope you enjoy this new (but old) biblical language for sex.

And feel free to laugh, with delight, surprise, or amusement.

apples: testicles

clusters (of the palm): breasts

dew: male sexual secretions

entering the garden: sexual intercourse

fawns: breasts

feed among the lilies: oral sex or sexual kissing

foxes: interruptions or obstacles to sex

fruit: genitals, male or female (usually female)

garden: vulva and vagina

garden of nuts: penis and testicles

gazelle: penis

know/knowing/known: sexual intercourse

lovesick: horny

mountains: breasts

myrrh: female sexual secretions

orchard of pomegranates: vulva and vagina

palm: woman's body

pleasant fruits: pleasure coming from the vagina—the Song likens entering the garden to entering paradise

round goblet: vulva

stag: penis, sometimes the whole male body

towers: breasts

twins of a gazelle: breasts

vine: penis, sometimes the whole body

vineyard: the woman's body or genitals

wine: symbol of erotic pleasure

You can use these words to make fun, sexy phrases that you and your wife share. Here are a few of our favorites:

"I think the stag is ready to play in the garden."

"I feel like getting some fruit from the orchard."

"The vine is definitely growing in the garden of nuts."

"I'm in the mood to climb the palm tree."

"We should let the gazelle and fawns out tonight."

"Would you like me to feed among the lilies?"

We could go on, but you get the idea.

Have fun with the language God gave us for sex in the Song of Songs. By using these words, we're reclaiming sex as something from God. We're showing the Puritans that it's okay to be playful and sexy. It's putting the pornographers on notice that the Bible has better words for sex than they do. And it's honoring God's gift of sex in its fullness—something sacred, erotic, and fun.

And one last idea: invite your wife to read the Song of Songs with you. It provides a wonderful model for passionate intimacy, something to which you can aspire. You can use the principles of the book to inform the ways you treat each other and to enrich your sex life. However, I recommend setting aside more time than usual for Bible study while reading the Song. Things might get hot. You could end up doing "life application" of biblical principles right away. I hope you do. Imagine God's delight as you use the Bible for foreplay.

2

Knowing the Myths
and the Truth

Sex is a powerful subject. How is it that we've relegated the
subject to pornographers and the dullest of minds?

Bono

Until I (SS) was sixteen, I thought my wife would be named Pam.
That's what a "gypsy" told me when she read my palm at a Hal-
loween party in second grade. For the next several years, I ignored girls
named anything but Pamela or some derivative. When at last I met a girl
named Pam at my church youth group, I pursued her with the confidence
that fate was on my side. When her college boyfriend threatened several
times to beat me up, I started to reconsider palm reading's accuracy in
predicting the moniker of one's spouse. After some sound biblical teaching
about fortune-telling (and gaining a few IQ points), I decided that palm
reading was a bunch of hooey. (By the way, my wife's name is Shelley, and

her parents never even considered naming her Pam.) Because I believed a myth about palm reading, I wasted a lot of time, frightened a teenage girl, and almost got beat up.

Myths do that type of thing. They send you down wrong paths and get you in trouble. This happens with sex all the time.

Your wife wants you to have discernment when it comes to sexuality. Sex is a mysterious and powerful thing. It scares people. As a result, people perpetuate myths and urban legends about sex to rein it in. Some are ridiculous (like masturbating can cause blindness) and easily ignored, but there are some widely accepted myths. We're going to debunk these myths and then look at some *truths* about sex that don't get the attention they deserve. Before becoming a spectacular lover, you need to separate truth from fiction when it comes to wisdom about sex. Misguided notions will hinder your sex life, but your wife will feel safer and have more fun with a man who knows the truth.

Myths

Our first three myths have to do with the male sex drive.

The Impact of Emotions

The first myth is: "*A man's sexuality has nothing to do with his emotions.*"

Theologian James Nelson said, "When the body is experienced as a *thing*, it has the right to live only as a machine or slave."[1] If you believe the messages in pop culture (and sometimes Christian culture), men aren't sentient beings when it comes to sex; we're machines. Just push a button and we spring to action, ready to perform like stallions at the first sign of a naked woman. Most men are more complicated than that. Several factors affect our sexuality.

The first one is self-esteem. When a man feels good about himself, he's more likely to have a healthy sex life. He'll have sexual interest in his wife without being needy and he'll enjoy sex. But when a man has a poor self-image or feels inadequate, his sexuality will suffer. For example, a man who thinks he's ugly or overweight might not show as much interest in sex because he's embarrassed (and you thought this only happened to women). A man who has no meaningful goals or purpose in life may turn to sex or pornography as an escape. The sex isn't even that good; it's just a distraction from feeling lost and hopeless.

In a similar way, a man's mood has an effect on his sexuality, but it's more temporary than the effect of his self-image. A man in a good mood is ready for great sex, but he'll be okay if he can't have it. This isn't true for men who are stressed out, depressed, angry, or fatigued. Such moods result in extreme attitudes about sex, causing men to either need it desperately or avoid it altogether. A bad mood is easier to overcome than poor self-esteem, but it still has an effect. It's just easier to push through a bad mood and manage some good sex. Being aware of how your mood affects your sexuality will go a long way toward promoting a better love life.

Performance anxiety harms a man's sexual experience more than almost anything. Whether it's pressure to maintain an erection, delay ejaculation, have a fast ejaculation, make a baby, or provide an orgasm for his wife, such demands make a man anxious and can rob him of intimacy and pleasure. This can result in frustration, resentment, and even sexual sin. Remember, the best sex is free from pressure.

Great lovers are marathon runners not sprinters. You're not going to be able to have mind-blowing sex at the flick of a switch. You need a lifestyle that promotes great sex always, rather than worrying about each individual experience. Understanding how your emotions affect your sex drive and performance will go a long way toward creating a fantastic sex life throughout your married life.

Men's Interest in Sex

"Men are more interested in sex than women." It's probably not quite fair to describe this as a myth because it's more socially acceptable for men

to express interest in sex. However, that's not always a reflection of the true level of sexual desire, especially among Christians who learn early to keep quiet about such things. Making matters more confusing, men and women often buy into the stereotypes. Men begin to think there's something wrong with them if they aren't horny all the time, and women may feel ashamed if they are.

Hormones, especially testosterone, play a significant part in sexual desire. Men have about five to ten times more testosterone than women do. This might lead you to believe that men have more sexual desire than women. However, women are more sensitive to testosterone than men. To make matters more confusing, the level of testosterone in a woman's body changes across her reproductive cycle. If you aren't lost by now, this next point should do the trick. *Different women* have *different levels* of sensitivity to testosterone, which changes depending on the time of the month. You might think you need some advanced calculus to figure this out, but all this means is that your wife may have less sexual desire than you or she may have more. It also means that sometimes your wife may have little sexual desire, while at other times she's an insatiable sex beast. And these are just the biological factors. Throw in the spiritual, psychological, and social variables, and any stereotypes we have for "all women" start to look ridiculous.

We can't assume much about our own sexual desires or those of our wife. Instead, we must communicate and learn. We find out what turns each other on and we don't take it personally when one of us isn't in the mood. We see each other as complex, intricately woven creations of God responding to a variety of factors. The more open you are about sexuality with your wife, the more you'll both learn. Sooner or later, that's going to make for some really great sex.

Boring Sex

"Sex with the same person gets boring." I once heard a stand-up comedian compare sex to cereal. He said that a single man who has sex with

multiple partners is like a man who eats a different kind of cereal every morning. Once a man is married, the comedian said, he has to eat the same type of cereal all the time.

For starters, anyone who can compare sex to eating cereal has never had great sex. Sex that can be likened to a box of cornflakes lacks emotional and spiritual intensity. The comedian was right in one sense—careless, selfish sex does get boring with the same person because it's focused on fulfilling physical urges instead of intense intimacy. If you're having sex only to gratify your sexual appetite, then sex is just like cereal—a dry, sugary substitute for a hot meal.

Sex with the same person gets boring only if the couple allow *the relationship* to get boring. Couples who strive for intimacy through the mundane rhythms of life won't experience sex as boring. People who have exciting sex with one partner for years work at keeping the relationship fresh and stay creative in the bedroom. In other words, if sex becomes boring, it's your own fault. Don't think for a second that a new sex partner won't become just as boring if *you* are boring in your approach to relationships. Emotional and spiritual intimacy makes for sex that never gets old.

Now let's clear up some myths about sexual practices.

Christians and Sex

"*Christians can't have wild sex.*" I've actually heard from the pulpit that Christians should stick to the missionary position. Here's the supposed logic behind this: if you aren't face to face with your wife while having sex, it's disrespectful and promotes lust instead of intimacy.

Intimacy has to do with a whole lot more than eye contact. It's a lifestyle, an attitude, a level of commitment, and a feeling of passion. It has very little to do with the mechanics of sex. If you aren't experiencing intimacy in all these intangible ways, having a staring contest during sex won't help.

But you know what does promote intimacy? Fun. You know what helps you have fun during sex? Adding variety and trying new things, like oral sex.

Oral sex and trying different sexual positions can promote just as much intimacy as the missionary position, sometimes more. When you try new things with your wife, not only will you have fun, but you will be making yourself vulnerable. You will be seeing each other from a different angle and exposing more of yourself—literally!

Trying new things to spice up your sex life means that you both feel safe enough to experiment. You love each other so much that it will be okay if something doesn't work or doesn't feel just right. You don't have to do everything perfectly and you're free to take some risks. Taking risks can lead to fun, and fun can lead to greater intimacy, which then leads to more fun (isn't this cool?).

But back to oral sex.

Oral sex is a powerful, vulnerable experience. It's a tragedy that secular culture, pornography in particular, has turned oral sex into something that emphasizes power and objectification. The devil really did a number on us by promoting oral sex as "dirty." In a loving, committed context, it's an amazing experience. It's trusting each other enough to release control in a very intimate way. It doesn't get much more intimate than "going down." This may be one of the reasons that some women can only experience orgasm through cunnilingus. When your wife allows you to go down on her, she's reached an extraordinary place of vulnerability, one that frees her to fully embrace the sexual experience. That, and it feels really good.

We'll get into more of the details on this stuff in chapter 9. For now, it's important to acknowledge that different sexual positions don't promote objectification and lust in a loving marriage. They take intimacy to a whole new level.

Masturbation

"Masturbation ruins sex with your wife." It's obligatory to deal with "the sin of Onan" when discussing masturbation, kind of like singing the national anthem before a baseball game. Let's get it out of the way.

Genesis 38:9–10 says, "But since Onan knew that the offspring would not be his, he spilled his semen on the ground whenever he went in to his brother's wife, so that he would not give offspring to his brother. What he did was displeasing in the sight of the LORD, and he put him to death also." Some base the belief that masturbation is a sin on this verse. Since Onan "spilled his semen"—meaning he pulled out when he ejaculated—he was sinning by wasting sperm. By this logic, masturbation is a sin because you're wasting sperm. However, most biblical scholars agree that Onan's sin was disobeying God's command to produce offspring for his brother's wife. In other words, wasting sperm alone wasn't Onan's sin, nor was it masturbation.

Masturbation, like so many things, *can* be a sin. It can be a destructive, addictive force that injures lives and relationships. In and of itself, however, it is neither good nor bad; it's a physiological event. (They say 95 percent of men masturbate, and the other 5 percent are lying.) If you stimulate your penis enough, you'll ejaculate. Whether it's sinful and damaging depends on your motivation, your thoughts, and the degree to which it becomes a habit. If you masturbate while having lustful or adulterous fantasies, it's sinful and sexually unhealthy (Matt. 5:28). It's objectifying to women and it will dull your capacity to enjoy intimacy with your wife. It can also become an unhealthy escape, making you avoid relationship problems rather than fixing them. Some men become so addicted to masturbation that they prefer it to sex with their wife. There's no question that, frequently, masturbation gets in the way of spiritual purity and healthy sexuality.

But sometimes it's not so bad. Occasional masturbation with pure thoughts or appropriate fantasies (loving sex with your wife, for example) won't hurt your sex life, and there's nothing in the Bible suggesting that it's sinful. In the following instances, masturbation can even be helpful:

+ *Premature ejaculation.* If you suffer from premature ejaculation, masturbating a couple hours before you have sex can prolong intercourse.

+ *Overactive libido.* Some men are "blessed" with an extra helping of testosterone. There's no way that their wives can keep up with them. If these guys masturbate minimally, they're doing their wives a favor and facilitating a much better sex life overall. They just need to be careful not to do it *more* than they have sex with their wives, so they don't begin to prefer it.

+ *Times of separation and illness.* When your wife is sick or the two of you are separated for a long period of time, masturbation can decrease sexual frustration and temptation. Just be sure to keep fantasies focused on your wife or altogether absent. And keep masturbation to an absolute minimum so it doesn't become a habit. Save it for when you feel like you're going nuts. Masturbation can be a good release as long as it doesn't lead to a preference for fantasy or pornography over the real thing. If you're separated for a short time, consider holding off and letting things "build up." It can set you up for an awesome time when you reunite.

If you're still unsure about masturbation, get an accountability partner to help you pay attention to your thought life and avoid pornography. In general, consider masturbation a last resort.

Active or Passive

"*In bed, men should be active, and women should be passive.*" Even though most people know this isn't true, many behave as if it is. Because of this myth, men often feel the burden of performance. They feel that the quality of every sexual experience is up to them. It's their job to make it great and their responsibility if it fails. Likewise, a woman may feel she isn't permitted to assert her desires during sex. She may feel that she has to wait on her husband rather than initiating sex.

This is a myth we can definitely live without. A lot of women would enjoy sex more if they could be more active. And I think it's safe to say their husbands would like it too. Men get more pleasure from sex if they don't feel the pressure to pursue and perform all the time. As we saw in the Song of Songs, the best sex is a mutual effort. It's fine for one person to initiate and take the lead, but it should feel like a shared experience.

Truths

Now that we've got some myths out of the way, let's look at some refreshing truths.

Overcoming the Past

"You can overcome a promiscuous past." It's crucial that Christians preach abstinence and do their best to practice it before marriage. It's also important to inform kids about the natural consequences of unprotected sex, such as pregnancy and sexually transmitted disease. But sometimes we go too far and we convince people that they are "damaged goods" if they've had premarital sex. I've encountered young men who believed that they were doomed to think of other women they'd slept with when they had sex with their future wife. I've met women who, after giving in to temptation once, gave up and continued to have sex because they saw sexual purity as an all or nothing proposition. A single moment of weakness may cause someone to think, *I've already blown it, so I might as well go ahead and keep having sex.* Such shame is not only counter to Christian grace, it defeats the purpose of preaching abstinence in the first place.

If you had sex before marriage, even if you were downright promiscuous, you can still have wonderful sex with your wife. You're not destined to think of that girl with whom you had a weak moment during spring break. You have to do two things to overcome a promiscuous past:

1. *Ask forgiveness and repent.* If you're single, that means you're waiting for marriage to have another sexual relationship. Whether you're

single or married, it means that you turn your back on your sexual past, accepting that it was sinful. This is harder than it sounds for some men, especially if they think the sex with previous women was *better* than it is with their wife. These guys have to realize that sex without lifelong commitment can never be the best sex. For reasons we'll discuss later, the best sex happens only in marriage. You have to accept that you settled for less before you were married and believe that the best sex is still ahead of you.

2. *Love your wife.* If you feel deep, passionate love for your wife and have sought forgiveness from God, there's no way you're going to be psychologically manhandled by past sexual sins. In fact, the only time that previous sexual experiences may cause trouble is when there are problems in the marriage or the man feels inhibited in loving his wife. This indicates a deeper problem with the marriage or the man. If that's the case, seek help from a Christian counselor.

Some women have promiscuous pasts as well. A man married to such a woman might worry that she compares him to old lovers and that he won't measure up. As long as his wife loves him passionately, he needn't worry. Remember, great sex isn't just about technique, it's about the intensity that intimacy creates. Even if your wife had sex with a guy nicknamed "Dr. Love," it won't matter as long as the two of you share emotional and spiritual passion. Past mistakes can't threaten that kind of connection. If Dr. Love enters her mind, it will only be as a lame comparison to the great lover she has now. A man preoccupied with his wife's past, despite the fact she loves him passionately, might be wrestling with his own issues of self-esteem or old wounds. He should seek help in overcoming these issues.

It is also important that you see your wife as a "virgin bride" regardless of her past. If she's asked forgiveness, she's clean of her sexual sins in the eyes of God. Isaiah 43:25 says, "I, even I, am he who blots out your transgressions, for my own sake, and remembers your sins no more" (NIV).

Psalm 103:12 says, "As far as the east is from the west, so far he removes our transgressions from us." In Jewish wedding traditions, the bride wears white whether she's a virgin or not, representing God's view of her as pure. When God looks at your wife, he doesn't see her sin. He sees a virgin. If God forgets her sins, who are you to hold them against her?

One more thing. It's not necessary for either of you to confess all the gory details of your past. It's good for couples to have a broad sense of each other's sexual history and get tested for STDs, but that's it. Giving each other names, dates, and explicit descriptions will only make things harder. Specific confession may be part of your repentance, but it isn't your wife you should tell. Honesty is not the same as transparency. You can leave out some details without deceiving your wife about the fact that you've made mistakes. Who you are now, with each other and before God, matters most. The two of you can know each other intimately and authentically without describing every weak moment. This leads us to our next little-known truth.

The Place for Confession

"Confession is good for the soul, but not always for the marriage." Confession of sexual sin to his wife often is what brings a man to our therapy offices. If she doesn't decapitate him on the spot, she makes him get into counseling. During the first session, we always surprise such a guy by asking him, "Why did you tell your wife?"

One of the myths in Christian culture is that redemption and recovery from sexual sin requires confession to your spouse. It's not in the Bible and there's no research that says it helps the marriage or recovery process. However, it's easy to understand how this notion became popular with Christians. Honesty is important to us, and we hate feeling guilty. If a Christian man sins against his wife through adultery or pornography, he may feel that he's deceiving his wife if he doesn't tell her, and that the deception is yet another sin. Most guys who confess to their wife feel that they're doing the right thing and that it's the first step on the path to repentance.

Nothing in the Bible mandates confessing sexual sin to your wife. It's one of those notions that sounds good on paper but don't always work in practice. I'm not saying that you should never tell your wife about sexual sin under any circumstance, but it's not always a good idea and sometimes it's a terrible one.

Let's say you have a problem with Internet pornography. If your wife is a very strong woman with abundant self-confidence and a compassionate heart, the best you can hope for is that she'll be devastated. She'll have a hard time trusting you, and intimacy will take months or longer to rebuild.

Though your wife's response is fair and appropriate, it will probably not help your problem with porn in the long run. You'll feel deservedly punished and it will deter you for a little while, but it will do nothing to get at the root problem. In some cases, your wife's anger, though justified, will make you feel more distant from her and make it harder to stay off the porn.

A man who's addicted to porn or in the midst of an affair may be overwhelmed with guilt and feel that telling his wife will relieve that guilt. Though he might feel better after a confession, his wife will feel much worse. His release from guilt will come at her expense. A man might also tell his wife because he thinks that it will force him to stop sinning. However, it will help only temporarily and, again, that help comes at great emotional cost to his wife.

If you struggle with addiction to pornography, you've had an affair, or you've committed some other sexual sin, you must address it. Begin by confessing to someone other than your wife—a close friend, a pastor, or a Christian therapist. Then commit to a program of recovery and healing. There may be a good reason for you to confess to your wife, but first seek the advice of someone else you trust. You may suffer more guilt as a result, but that's part of the price you pay. If you decide that it's important to tell your wife, be prepared to support her in patience and love as she begins the long road of rebuilding trust. It's neither fair nor realistic for a man to expect his wife to get over it quickly, no matter how repentant he is.

If you choose not to tell your wife, that doesn't make it okay to keep living a lie. We're not advocating keeping things a secret from your wife and *continuing* to do them. You have to commit to change, or things will get worse.

If that depressed you, this next truth should cheer you up.

Time with the Guys

"*Time with the guys will improve sex with your wife.*" A recent study found that a man's testosterone level decreases when he's in a romantic relationship but increases when he spends time with other guys.[2] A few hours hanging out with the guys will increase your desire for your wife. God made us so that time with other men makes us long for the woman we love. Explain this to your wife the next time she protests when you want to play basketball with the guys.

It's not just the hormones, however. Something about being around other guys refreshes, refines, and solidifies our masculine identity, like iron sharpening iron (see Prov. 27:17). You have certain needs that your wife can't meet, a way of relating that only other men understand. For example, I can talk to Rick and Ryan about things that would amuse our wives for about ninety seconds. After that, they think we're dorks. But we crack each other up and get to enjoy enthusiasm for similar interests. Often, when men hang out with other men, they leave each other feeling more whole and in a better position to meet the needs of their wives. If your wife understands that, she'll be more than happy to let you take off to watch the game or go camping once in a while.

Sex and Marriage

Now we reach our favorite little-known truth: *"Sex can help other aspects of a marriage (and vice versa!)."* Sometimes a client will come to us and say, "Sex is the only thing holding my marriage together." We always respond by saying, "Good! At least something is, and this particular something is pretty resilient."

A lot of folks regard sex as a fringe benefit to marriage, something recreational unless it's done for the sake of procreation. On the contrary, sex is an essential part of marriage. We don't mean that something is wrong if you're not having sex five times a week, but it should be an important part of your relationship just like communication, parenting, or financial planning. If you have a healthy sex life, there's a good chance that other areas of your relationship will be stable.

You can do an experiment to see how this works. Pick a typical area of conflict with your wife, anything from taking out the trash to finances. The next time you have sex, discuss that area of conflict afterward. Don't even bother to get dressed. The discussion is almost certain to go better than it did before. It's not just because the physical release of sex has made you more relaxed (though that doesn't hurt). Sex can make a man and wife feel closer, like the "one flesh" they really are. The intimacy creates a bond that holds against stress and conflict. In fact, if you have regular knockdown, drag-out fights right after sex, something is wrong with your marriage, and you need to seek professional help.

Though sex is crucial to a stable marriage, it can't do the job alone. There are many other areas of intimacy and collaboration that need attention. But the cool thing is that nurturing other areas of your relationship facilitates a great sex life. This is especially true for women. Many times, a man can put aside frustration about something to have sex, but it may be harder for his wife to do this. If she's upset about yesterday's argument, it will be more of a challenge for her to have good sex. Be aware that even the most mundane aspects of your relationship affect your sex life. If you can remember that, you may be more sensitive the next time you and your wife butt heads after you've left the toilet seat up.

Orgasms

"*Orgasms are* not *necessary for great sex, not even your own.*" Sex is an experience to be relished, not a sporting event where the winner has the best orgasm. We'll get into this more in chapter 9. For now, avoid treating sex like a football game where you're the quarterback, your wife is a defensive linebacker, a touchdown is your wife's orgasm, and the extra-point kick is yours.

The Mystery of Sex

Part of the allure of sex is its mystery. It's something that goes on in private. It holds secrets. That's good and we don't want to yank back the covers and rob sex of its mystery entirely. You and your wife should make discoveries and have secrets that no one else knows about. Sex should be mysterious but not confusing. Dispelling myths and uncovering the truth about sex can reduce confusion and anxiety and equip you for a healthier sex life. The secular world already tells too many lies about sex. As Christians, it's our job to unveil the truth about sex.

But we have to do more than warn people about the bad parts. We need to reveal what makes for a fun, healthy, and vibrant sex life. Imagine what would happen if Christians became known as the experts on great sex. We would steal pornography's market and show the world that Puritan rigidity isn't Christian.

In the U2 concert film *Rattle and Hum*, Bono introduces U2's version of the Beatles' song "Helter Skelter" by saying, "Charles Manson stole this song from the Beatles, and we're stealing it back." The pornographers and Puritans have stolen sex from Christians with their lies. When we know the truth about sex, we're stealing it back.

PART TWO

Knowing
Yourself

3

Knowing How to Be a Man

For this reason a man will leave his father and mother and
be united to his wife.

Genesis 2:24 NIV

Imagine a man and his wife driving away from their wedding reception
. . . with the man's mother in the backseat. It sounds ridiculous, but
it happens all the time. Every weekend grooms drive off from their wedding like this, still boys instead of men. Years later we see some of these
husbands in marital therapy, wondering why their marriage turned into
such a bad road trip. Still others drove their marriages over a cliff even
before they made it in to see us. If you want to have a successful future
with your wife, you have to leave your mother—and your father—behind
at your wedding.

Although it is quoted in many Jewish and Christian weddings, many
husbands forget God's timeless and wise prescription for a good mar-

riage: "For this reason a man will leave his father and mother and be united to his wife" (Gen. 2:24 NIV). This isn't just a nice sounding Scripture verse for wedding ceremonies. It's God's prerequisite for loving your wife. Before you drive off with your wife, you have to drop off your parents.

A man needs to grow up, leave his mom and dad, and become his own man if he wants to be a great lover to his wife. If you want any further confirmation of this, just have your wife or girlfriend read that last sentence. You can tell what she's thinking if she is nodding her head or shouting, "Amen!" She might even jump up and down with tears in her eyes, saying, "Yes! No more mama's boy!" We're just warning you. When a man remains tied to his mommy's apron strings, he will still be trying to please his mom and he won't have his own separate identity with his wife. Likewise, a man who feels his father's abandonment or disapproval will carry deep insecurities about ever being "enough" of a man for his wife.

Are your parents still sitting in the backseat of your marriage? When you hear your wife offer suggestions, are you really hearing your mother's voice? Do you react with automatic compliance—or resistance—because you still feel like a boy around women? And when you make a wrong turn or mistake in life, do you still hear your father's voice saying, "What's wrong with you? Are you stupid?" If your parents are still in the backseat, it's time to pull over and drop them off. A man needs to be free from his parents before he can drive anywhere with his wife.

Learning the lovemaking techniques later in this book will be meaningless if you still feel like a boy, act like a boy, and think like a boy. Sound familiar to you? Paul said the same thing when he wrote the most eloquent description of love in literary history. "When I was a child, I talked like a child, I thought like a child, I reasoned like a child. When I became a man, I put childish ways behind me" (1 Cor. 13:11 NIV). Only a man can love the way Paul describes in this chapter. As you read these next four verses on love, ask yourself if a boy could love like this (think of playboys while you're at it). "Love is patient, love is kind. It does not envy, it does not boast, it is not proud. It is not rude, it is not self-seeking, it is not easily angered, it keeps no record of wrongs. Love does not delight in evil but rejoices with the truth. It always protects, always trusts, always hopes, always perseveres" (vv. 4–7 NIV). If you don't love like this, it could mean that you still have some growing up to do. In fact, loving like this will help you grow up.

Now that you have just read Paul's master definition of love, be a man and memorize this passage. If you are serious about being a great lover, you need to bury this biblical prescription for love in your heart. Think about your marriage in relation to this passage at least once a week. If you are a checklist kind of guy, go ahead and use it as a checklist. This is how a man loves his wife. It's how Jesus loves us.

Our Peter Pan Culture of Perpetual Boyhood

Today Christian men struggle in their marriages nearly as much as non-Christian men. The reason for this is that our culture is dedicated to keeping men from growing up. Currently the typical role models for younger men are men who still act like adolescents. At over eighty years old, Hugh Hefner has lived his entire life as a boy. By relating to women as a playing boy, Hef has never loved a woman like a man. Yet Hefner has had a profound influence on shaping our culture's view of manhood (or boyhood).

Our forefathers had meaningful standards for masculinity. Character qualities such as courage, integrity, fidelity, and hard work were common ideals that men strove to achieve. Such standards are foreign to most men today. Our culture is so confused about what makes for true masculinity that even many Christian men act like adolescents at age forty. The following chart (adapted from a greeting card) illustrates the common stages of a man's life.

Seven Stages of a Man's Life

Age	Stage
0–1	infancy
2–4	toddlerhood
5–12	childhood
13–19	early adolescence
20–39	adolescence
40–54	middle adolescence
55+	late adolescence

This chart isn't that far from reality for a lot of men. We're not saying that acting like a teenager is always a bad thing. The most mature men act like adolescents sometimes. It can be fun and there's nothing wrong with that, but if it's the only way a guy can relate to women, his wife will eventually wish that she had married a man instead of a teenage boy.

Peter Pan is one of the best men's books ever written about the refusal to grow up. It illustrates the clear choice that men face of remaining a boy or becoming a man. To avoid growing up, Peter Pan escapes from adult reality to spend his life in Neverland with the Lost Boys. Although the book is a fairy tale, there are millions of men doing the same thing today, and that includes millions of Christian Lost Boys too. If you're ready to leave Neverland for the promised land of a great love life, it's time to make a choice. God is calling you to become a man. You couldn't give your wife a better wedding or anniversary present. The first step is saying good-bye to your mother.

Leaving Your Mother

When a man has difficulty with committing himself to a woman, often it's because he felt smothered or controlled by his mother as a boy. His fear is that he will repeat the same experience with his wife (as if he is helpless to do anything about it!). For those men who do marry, they may try to control, intimidate, or hurt their wife's feelings to ensure that no woman will ever dominate them again. Other men who felt guilty for ever hurting their mother will try to avoid any arguments and disagreements with their wife. They comply with their wife just as they complied with their mother.

Men obsessed with pornography or prostitutes may also have some unfinished business with their mother. Old feelings of anger, guilt, or fear are often unconscious motivators for men to turn to women whom they can "control" in fantasy. Real relationships with real women can feel too threatening. We've heard from single men who say they actually prefer pornography to real women. Such cowardice reflects that they never became real men.

A man's first relationship with a woman, his mother, has a profound effect on how, as an adult, he relates to women. If his mother is secure, consistent, affirming, and respectful, and loves his father, a boy can leave home well prepared to love a woman as a man. In fact, he will choose a wife with the same mature qualities. But if a boy's mother is insecure, nervous, anxious, depressed, possessive, unpredictable, withdrawn, threatening, seductive, or controlling, or if she hates men . . . well, you get the picture, and it's not pretty. Mothers like these prepare a boy to experience fear, avoidance, shame, and rage in his relationships with women. If a man doesn't leave behind the wounds from the relationship with his mother, he will carry them with him into his future relationships.

Hugh Hefner is a perfect example. His unresolved relationship with his mother ruined his sex life. Instead of loving a woman as a man and a husband, Hef has kept his distance from women by playing with them like toys. When he was a boy, Hefner says, his mother was cold and rarely touched him. "There was no affection of any kind, and I escaped to dreams and fantasies."[1] Instead of getting over his pain and growing up to be a man, he remains a hurting boy. Hefner chose the Peter Pan life as a way of coping with his pain. Surrounding himself with more breasts than any man in history, Hef found a compromise. He would get validation of his worth from women sexually, yet he would not love or depend on anyone in return (although he tried and failed at marriage twice—usually boys don't succeed at marriage). Hefner played it safe with women. He never let himself be hurt again.

Hef is not alone. Millions of men use pornography to keep their distance from real women. The allure of pornography is that a man can feel close to a woman and yet remain emotionally separated from her at the same time. For men who had controlling, distant, angry, or dependent mothers, the temptation to use pornography can be especially great. The promise of women in pornography is that they will never frustrate, control, or disappoint. Like the Victoria's Secret angels, these models aren't seen as human—they are out of this world—nearly divine. Men who haven't separated from their mothers can easily turn to fantasies and the safe embrace of unreal women. This embrace has no apron strings attached, but it's the loneliest embrace in the world.

Men can also feel like lonely little boys in their marriages. Mike was this kind of husband. He had been married for twelve years, "the twelve unhappiest years of my life," before coming to therapy. He said that his wife had refused to have sex with him for the past three years, belittled him around their friends and at church, and wouldn't "let him" have any time away from her. As he talked about his boyhood, Mike began to see some pieces come together. "As I think about it, my wife is a lot like my mother. My mom put my dad down all the time, and she never loved us kids either. She told us all the time that she didn't want to be a mother and couldn't wait until we grew up and left home. The truth is, my wife treats me a lot like my mom treated me." And the deeper truth was that Mike allowed himself to be treated like that. Since he never resolved his wounds from his mother, Mike believed that he deserved to be the target of a woman's wrath. He put up with his wife's never-ending resentment because he expected her criticism. He may even have provoked his wife to resent him. He feared his wife like a boy who fears an angry mother.

Mike needed the help of a man to separate from his mother and become his own man. A father would be the obvious person to play this role. Unfortunately, Mike never met his father. But even if a boy has a father, the mother still plays a significant role by how willing she is to let her son identify with his father. The way the mother treats the father will influence the boy's motivation to identify with him.[2]

Boys raised only by their mother have a harder time feeling secure and confident about their manhood. A boy needs his dad to identify with his masculine gender. He needs a father who welcomes him into the world of men. The problem for so many boys today is that they don't have a dad around to do this. In fact 40 percent of boys in our country will go to bed tonight without their father in the house. This epidemic wreaks havoc in men's lives and marriages.

Since so many boys did not grow up with their father, it is no wonder that divorce is so common today. As one client said, with his head buried in his hands, "I didn't want to be a mama's boy! But what choice did I have? My dad left when I was seven, and my mother never remarried. It's like she made me her substitute husband." Feeling inferior and insecure around other men, this man later turned to gambling and pornography for the validation of his manhood that he never received from a father. Of course, it didn't help. When boys are left on their own to define their manhood, usually they will not succeed.

The film *Boyz in the Hood* depicted this desperation in the lives of young black men in South Central Los Angeles. Mostly boys without fathers, they're left on their own to become men. The director, John Singleton, later made a sequel called *Baby Boy*, which graphically illustrates the conflict between adult men who never grow up and the women they desire. During a love scene between Jody, the main character, and his girlfriend, the two growl at each other over and over again, "I love you, I hate you. I love you, I hate you." As Singleton explains, "This is a movie about a generation of young black men who haven't grown up. They've all been raised by women, so they're always trying to show how much of a man they are, when what they really are is baby boys." He sees these gang members as young lions on the Serengeti Plain, except "they're going around the Crenshaw Mall, checking out the sixteen-year-old girls. They're trying to define and defend their manhood at the same time, from their women, the white world and themselves."[3]

Without fathers around to affirm and validate their masculinity, boys will often turn to bravado, toughness, or hyper-masculinity to prove that they are men. While they love their mothers, they are also angry that their mothers didn't give them a father. Hip-hop and rap lyrics often reflect this kind of rage at women. Domestic violence and sexual degradation of women are also common reflections of this angry and insecure masculinity. Boys desperately need fathers to validate their manhood. They have a basic need to identify with their father's masculinity and grow up to become a man like him.

So why does the Bible say that a man should *leave* his father before uniting with a wife?

Leaving Your Father

A man leaves his father in a different way than he leaves his mother. When a man leaves his mother, it means that he no longer depends on her as a boy depends on a woman. A son needs to leave his dependency on his father too, but he needs to take with him his father's basic masculinity. Also, ideally, he needs to leave with his father's blessing.

Millions of men don't leave their dads on good terms. Instead of identifying with their father's manhood, they leave resenting him. When fathers abuse drugs or alcohol, have fits of rage, overcriticize, physically abuse their sons, or withhold their pride and love, the result is bitterness. We know Christian men who so despised their father's uncontrolled sexuality and promiscuity that they felt ashamed of their *own* sexual desires—even for their wives! This was John's story. Even when his wife would comment about a beautiful actress on TV, John wouldn't let himself say anything. When his wife wore something sexy to bed, he would still not express all of his sexual passion for her. He felt bad about having sexual feelings because his father had cheated on his mother "with at least four but maybe more" women during his boyhood. John loved his wife, but he couldn't make love to her. He felt such resentment toward his father that he didn't want to be anything like him, including the way his father handled his sexuality. John shared his mother's belief that all men were like dogs.

Through some hard work in therapy, these beliefs began to change. John learned that he could be a man, like his dad, but a different kind of man. Eventually John was able to accept himself and his own "doglike" passions and could finally unleash them with his wife.

Men *do* have a nature that is not much different from male animals, but that doesn't make them shameful or bad. We have a lot in common with cocks, bucks, bulls, rams, and stags. Like these males, we have a higher level of testosterone than females do. The male sexual drive is not a bad thing at all. What matters is where you steer it. If you don't like how your father steered his sexual desires, then decide to steer yours in a different course. Do what you can to forgive your dad and get over your anger. Whether he was out of control with his sexual desires or didn't seem to have any, your mandate is to leave him and become your own man. Accept your own maleness as good, and be free to love your wife as the loving stag that God meant you to be.

Many fathers fail to be positive role models for their sons because they never became men themselves. If your father acted like an irresponsible adolescent and constantly hurt or failed those around him, it's because *his* father never helped him become a man. But even if your father didn't help you, you can still grow up and become a man anyway. The good news is that a man isn't dependent on his father to become a man. Other men can fill that void. As a Christian, you've got plenty of brothers ready to step up and help.

Your New Fraternity: The Iron Men

College fraternities are usually places where men continue to behave like boys, but Christian men have a different kind of fraternity. Proverbs 27:17 is the motto for this fraternity: "As iron sharpens iron, so one man sharpens another" (NIV).

In Hebrew, the verse actually reads, "so one man sharpens the face of his friend." In Middle Eastern and Eastern cultures, "face" relates to one's character. Christian brothers can sharpen each other's character and manhood. To grow and succeed, men need other men, and churches can be a great place for this kind of Iron Man training.

Boys need men to initiate them into manhood. In all the male rites of passage throughout the world, the older men of the tribe initiate the younger boys into manhood. It takes men to initiate men. Boys who think that they will become a man by having sex with a woman are misguided. Women can't initiate a boy into manhood, because a boy needs to identify himself with men—not women. As author Robert Bly observes: "Women can change the embryo to a boy, but only the men can change the boy to a man. Initiators say that boys need a second birth, this time a birth from men."[4] Christian men receive a second birth through Christ himself. As Jesus said, "You must be born again" (John 3:7 NIV). To believe in him is to have a new life as a man. And Jesus gives you many brothers to keep you growing in that new life.

To start up your own Iron Man fraternity, we suggest that you ask one or more Christian men to join you in a men's group. Commit to meet together every week or every other week. A consistent time and place usually helps everyone to keep their commitment. My own group of men (RR) met every Friday morning in the back corner of a restaurant for years. You could ask other men from your church's men's ministry, or you could invite some other Christian friends that you know and respect. Once you have started your men's group, a good way to begin is to study a book together. To grow in your masculine sexuality, your men could read a chapter of this book each week for thirteen weeks, or whatever variation of chapters that your group might decide. Your men can also find a good selection of other men's books at your local Christian bookstore or at Christianbooks.com.

Besides book studies, you can also simply discuss your men's relationships with their fathers, mothers, wives, girlfriends, or children. Whatever the book or topic that you use, the most important point is to regularly discuss how each of you is doing in your lives as Christian men. In my own group, I always start by asking if any of the men have a presssing need or issue that needs to be talked out first. Be sure to put aside the book study or planned topic if one of your men has a more urgent need to talk about something else. Finally, close your meeting by praying to the One who makes you a fraternity of brothers in the first place. God is committed to meeting all of your needs as a man. Your earthly father may not have given you all that you needed from him, but you have another Father who will.

Your Other Father

Your dad is not your only father. Here's some news for you: "To all who received him, to those who believed in his name, he gave the right to become children of God—children born not of natural descent, nor of human decision or a husband's will, but born of God" (John 1:12–13 NIV). You've had a second birth. You have another Father. Jesus revealed your other Father more than two thousand years ago. The scene was similar to the one in *The Empire Strikes Back* where Darth Vader reveals himself to his son, saying, "Luke, I am your father." Jesus did the same thing with Thomas and Philip (though under better circumstances). When Philip asked, "Lord, show us the Father and that will be enough for us," Jesus answered: "Anyone who has seen me has seen the Father. . . . I am in the Father and the Father is in me" (John 14:8–9,11 NIV). Philip wasn't expecting that answer. He didn't realize that he was already looking at the Father. Even Christian men often fail to realize this today.

If your father deserted you as a boy, your other Father says, "I will never leave you nor forsake you" (Josh. 1:5 NIV). If you never knew your father or his love, Jesus says, "He who loves me will be loved by my Father, and I too will love him and show myself to him" (John 14:21 NIV). As a Christian man, you have a Father who loves you, has time for you, and makes himself known to you. He also gives you his blessing.

Every man longs to hear his father's blessing. No man wants to guess if his father loved him or was proud of him. The same was true for Jesus. Even though his father Joseph had died, Jesus had his other Father to bless him and be with him. His other Father wasn't the silent type. At his baptism and transfiguration, Jesus's Father told him what every man wants to hear from his dad: "You are my Son, whom I love; with you I am well pleased" (Luke 3:22 NIV). In other words, his Father said, "I love you and I'm proud of you." Since you are the Father's adopted son, he says the same to you. If you never heard it from your dad, just listen to your other Father.

As you follow the Bible's design to leave your father and mother, you leave with your Father's blessing. And you leave with the model of the perfect Christian man—Christ Jesus himself.

Your Model of the Greatest Lover in the World

After visiting Jerusalem with his parents, Jesus did something that nearly gave them a heart attack. He ditched them—for three days. When Joseph and Mary found him back in the temple, Mary asked him, "Son, why have you treated us like this?" His answer should be our answer: "Why were you searching for me? Didn't you know I had to be in my Father's house?" (see Luke 2:41–51). Jesus left his mother and father and became his own man that day. Although he returned home with his family, Mary and Joseph knew that his dependency on them would soon be over. At age twelve, Jesus was already becoming a man.

God didn't intend for you to be a Peter Pan or a mama's boy. You're not meant to be a playboy or a Lost Boy. Your mandate is to leave your parents and love your wife as Christ loved the church. Your wife needs a man, not a boy, for a husband. We hate hearing wives say, "I have three children—my two kids and my husband," even when it's said in jest. Make sure that your wife never has reason to say this. Christian men should never be mistaken for boys.

When you say good-bye to your parents, let them know that you will always love them. Leave them with hugs and kisses if you want. But after you are married, your wife is your number one. Your journey and destiny are with her now. Love her like a Christian man and drive away with her into the greatest love life in the world. Make it a great trip!

4

Knowing Your Body
and Your Wife's Body

Do you remember the time your dad sat down with you and told you about the birds and the bees? How proudly he welcomed you into manhood, sharing his wisdom regarding the joys and pitfalls common to your newly acquired status? Remember how you left the conversation with a closer bond with your father, a deep respect and awe for the powerful gift of sex, and a genuine excitement about the prospect of trying it out? Remember?

No?

You're not alone. If you're like 90 percent of the men we've met, that talk never happened. If you're among the remaining "lucky" 10 percent, you probably had a talk that was some combination of awkward and hilarious. We've heard plenty. A few examples:

Dad: Son, your mother thinks I should tell you about sex. You probably
    already know everything from your friends, don't you?
Son: Yup.
Dad: Good. That settles it then.

—∿∿—

Dad: You're going to get interested in girls, and you're going to want to sleep with them, and they might want to sleep with you. Understand?

Son: So what about it?

Dad: Don't do it.

Son: Why?

Dad: Because I said so!

Son: What if I do?

Dad: No driving until you're eighteen. Got it?

Son: I guess so.

—∿∿—

Dad: I need to tell you about something. When a man and woman love each other very much, that love makes a baby.

Son: How does love make a baby? I mean, how does love become a baby in Mom's belly?

Dad: Well, the man just sticks his love right in there, and it becomes a baby.

Son: How? Like a needle giving her a shot?

Dad: Uh, something like that.

So you fumbled through puberty and adolescence, learning about sex through dirty jokes and stolen glimpses of *Penthouse*. Teenage guys talk about sex, but it's not always accurate. One man said to me: "Until I was fifteen, my friends and I thought a woman performs oral sex on a man, she swallows his semen, and nine months later she poops out a baby." These myths are far too common.

If anything, you probably learned more about female sexuality than your own. Movies, pornography, talk shows, and locker-room talk all focus on female anatomy and sexuality. You've been flooded with data

about the G-spot and other erogenous zones and have very little idea
how your own junk works.

In spite of the pornographers' efforts, most men don't know much
about how to make love to a woman. Even Sigmund Freud once said:
"The great question . . . which I have not been able to answer . . . is, 'What
does a woman want?'" Men rack their brains trying to figure women
out, but they will never completely understand women, and perhaps
they never should. I'm pretty sure God had this in mind when he created men to be forever driven to solve the mystery, and women to be a
forever unsolvable mystery. Women are the itch men can't quite scratch,
and that's how it should be.

Trying to scratch that itch, however, is more tolerable if a man has
a working knowledge of sexual biology. Schools teach sex education
around seventh grade. That's when boys have the attention span of a
goldfish. Most of them won't use what they learn for several years. Now
that you have greater concentration and motivation, let's do a refresher
course.

Meet Your Penis

First Things First

Quit worrying about penis size, though we don't blame you for having
a complex. Your email box is full of messages telling you it's too small.
Offers of pills, penis pumps, and fat-injection surgery sell you a myth of
your inadequacy. But we invite you to turn on your brain for a minute.
Consider these three facts:

1. *Quality matters more than quantity.* Only the first three inches of the
   vagina benefit from stimulation, so you don't need much more than
   that. When it comes to mutual sexual pleasure, penis length and
   girth mean nothing compared to the quality of foreplay, the sensitivity of touch, and the depth of intimacy in the relationship.

2. *All penises are basically the same size.* Ninety percent of all penises are around six inches when erect. One in twenty are a little smaller; one in twenty are a little bigger. Most men aren't hung like a horse.

3. *Nobody cares.* Consider the possibility that this whole area of interest is worthless. Why is it that so much attention is given to penis size, while very little is given to vagina size? Why compare yours to those of other guys? What do you think penis size really means? Is a guy with a bigger penis really more of a man? Irrational thinking abounds when it comes to the size of your vine. It's best to accept and appreciate what you have.

You probably want a big penis because all the older guys in the locker room had a bigger penis than yours. You were small and wanted to be big. As you grew, so did your penis, and now it's the same size as all those guys in the locker room. So put that worry to bed.

A Brief History of Your Penis

Your penis is that terribly important hotdog-looking appendage between your legs. You had to develop that penis—really. There was no guarantee you were going to have one. All embryos begin with female sex organs. Within the first few weeks of life, all sex organs are internal, and males are indiscernible from females. That's why expectant parents need to wait until the second trimester to have an ultrasound—the future stud fetus's manhood isn't visible until then. Even in the womb, your masculinity was an achievement.

When you were born, your penis was huge, red, swollen, and out of proportion to the rest of your body. Your dad and uncles jabbed each other in the ribs and said, "He's a boy, and *what* a boy he is!" Within the first few days, your parents decided whether or not to have you circumcised. Circumcision is the removal of excess foreskin (prepuce) that covers the round head (glans) of the penis. The vast majority of American-born men reading this book were circumcised, but that statistic is changing. Hygiene was a major concern during circumcision's heyday. Now that people generally shower daily and use soap, there's not as much need for circumcision.

When you were a little kid, you noticed that touching your penis sometimes felt good. If you did this in view of a parent, he or she probably commented on that touching. This was your first message about sexuality. Imagine this scenario: Three-year-old Junior reaches down to pick up a dropped Cheerio and finds his penis instead. He grabs it and starts to rub it for a minute. Junior's hypersensitive mother gasps in horror, slaps his hand, and shouts: "Don't you *ever* touch yourself like that again! That is a dirty, bad place, and I don't ever want to see you touching there!" This was recalled by one of my clients, but numerous men have similar stories.

So what message does this send Junior? His penis is bad and dirty, touching it is bad, deriving pleasure from the penis is bad, and, furthermore, if he's going to enjoy this little pleasure, by all means keep it away from mom. She'll freak out. It's forbidden fruit.

Not everyone has this reaction to boys exploring their bodies. Some men heard some variation of: "That feels good, but we don't touch ourselves there in front of others." Or better yet, "That's right! You're a boy with a penis and I'm proud of you! Someday you'll be a man and you'll use that penis to make yourself and a woman very happy." Early messages about sexuality can have a lasting impact. You may have to challenge these childhood messages as an adult. This is an important step toward gaining freedom from shame.

In your preteen years, your penis remained relatively dormant, used only for peeing, writing your name in the snow, or perhaps in an innocent game of "show me yours and I'll show you mine." Many men have shame surrounding their curiosity about their own and other boys' penises. Boys are just curious about what they've been forbidden to see. They want to know that what they've got hidden is the same as what other boys have.

Once they have that reassurance, it's on to bigger and better things, like burning ants with a magnifying glass or digging a hole to China.

Next, you're twelve to fifteen years old and having a crazy sexual dream, when boom! Something sort of painful, sort of exciting, and definitely sticky happens. Welcome to puberty—it's your first wet dream. You may have enjoyed this nocturnal emission enough to begin taking matters into your own hands. Whether it was a day and night free-for-all, a tortured cold war, or a peaceful coexistence, you had to forge a relationship with this new member in your life. Your penis was the portal to prompt pleasure and peace—a temporary escape into erotic fantasy, as well as a brief refuge from the anxiety, confusion, and stress of that life stage.

How much influence your penis has had on your life, including how it influenced your identity and relationships with your wife and God, varies from man to man. Regardless, it's had a tremendous impact on your masculine identity.

Somehow, you and your penis survived this tortuous developmental journey. Now let's go meet your dance partner.

Also Starring Her Vagina

The vagina is where your penis goes. It is between her legs, is about seven inches deep, and, due to muscular contractions, can vary in width from completely closed to large enough to pass a nine-pound mammal. This brings us back to the penis size absurdity. Do you really think another inch longer or thicker will make that much of a difference? Furthermore, most women report sharp pain when the penis hits the cervix. As we noted earlier, the first three inches of the vagina are the most sensitive, because the majority of nerve endings are there, making this part of the vagina the most responsive to stimulation.

The clitoris is the most sensitive section of the female genitalia. Located outside the vagina, hidden under a hood near the top of the labia (the "lips" on the vagina's exterior), the clitoris is the feminine equivalent

of the penis when it comes to sensitivity. Remember when I was talking about how all genitalia is female for the first twelve weeks? Yup, the
clitoris is the female counterpart to the penis. So pay it some attention
when you engage in foreplay and have sex. You wouldn't want your penis
ignored, would you?

And yes, there is a G-spot. The name is short for Grafenberg spot, but
due to a considerable lack of sexiness, the "rafenberg" part was dropped.
It's a patch about a centimeter wide about two inches into the vagina, on
the front (belly button) side of the vagina. When stimulated, this spot has
been shown to increase the frequency and intensity of orgasms.

Speaking of orgasms, women can have more than one per encounter.
While men require a period of downtime between climaxes, many women
remain in the plateau phase (see under Sexual Response Cycle below)
through several orgasms. Peeing standing up and the ability to recite
every line from *Hoosiers* are nice achievements, but ladies get multiple
orgasms and seven more years on earth to enjoy them.

Some females also ejaculate. Ten percent of women have orgasms
accompanied by fluid expulsion, believed to be glandular and not urine,
from the urethra. Many men love this unique "proof" of orgasm.

The mysteries of female sexuality are too numerous to describe. Not
even the women themselves have the answers. This seems to be part of
God's plan. If we could figure out this mystery, we might not remain as
interested. A blank crossword puzzle keeps your interest more than one
that's filled in. So accept not knowing, but keep trying to find out. That's
part of the beautiful journey of marriage.

Erogenous Zones

Not only do men and women have all this interesting, unique equip-
ment, there are many places on their bodies that produce pleasure when
touched. A caress, massage, kiss, or gentle tickle can stir the embers for
passionate lovemaking. Check out this list, and add a few if you wish:

Male and Female Erogenous Zones

ears	feet
neck	back of knees
lips	thighs
eyelids	buttocks
back of neck	mind (poetry, erotica, etc.)
nipples	_____ (fill in the blank)
breasts	

The Sexual Response Cycle

Okay, now that we know the parts, let's figure out what happens when they're put together. The important issues of love, intimacy, and foreplay will come in later chapters. Here we're just learning the basics. Let's start with the five stages of the *sexual response cycle*.

Sexual Response Cycle

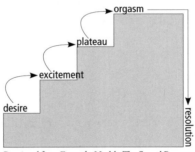

Reprinted from EngenderHealth, The Sexual Response Cycle, 2003.

Stage 1: Desire

Most people describe desire as being "turned on"—it's the signal that our brain is aware of sexual stimuli. Our mind and body respond to a variety of stimuli—including sight, sound, smell, touch, taste, movement, fantasy, and memory. These stimuli can create *sexual desire*—a strong yearning for sexual stimulation or sexual intimacy. The stimuli that spark sexual desire are different for everyone, and responses to varied stimuli are affected by feelings, thoughts, interests, and past experiences. In addition to individual preferences, societal and cultural values influence what types of stimuli are acceptable or favored by groups of people. For example, in mainstream American culture, scantily clad lingerie models are considered sexy, while in other areas of the world, a woman's clothed body is far more intriguing and inspires sexual desire.

What we're saying is that everyone has different ways of getting turned on. It helps to be able to identify the types of stimuli that spark sexual desire in you.

Indications of desire. Desire is based in the mind, and occurs before physical arousal. Sexual desire can be experienced as a fleeting thought or fantasy that may not lead to physical sexual excitement. Desire can be communicated verbally or through body language and behavior, such as flirting. You may have a special look or phrase that you use to tell your wife that you desire her. Again, desire doesn't necessarily lead to a sexual encounter, but it can be helpful to let your partner in on what sparks your fire.

Stage 2: Excitement

Sexual excitement (or arousal) is the body's physical response to desire. Some males, especially teenagers, reach the excitement stage with little physical or mental stimulation. As men get older, it can take more intense stimuli to move from the desire stage to physical excitement. In general it takes a bit longer for women to achieve full physical arousal. (In case you missed this point, take note. If you're moving toward a sexual encounter, you may need to be patient while your wife catches up to your level of physical arousal.) Excitement may lead to physical intimacy and sexual activity, but this is not inevitable. For both sexes, initial physical excitement may be lost and regained many times without progression to the next stage. In fact, an experience of desire and excitement that doesn't lead immediately to a sexual encounter can build anticipation and increase the intensity of the lovemaking when it does occur.

Indications of excitement. For both men and women there are certain indicators of sexual arousal.

+ *For both sexes:* Heart rate and blood pressure rise; body muscles tense; sexual flush occurs; nipples become erect; genital and pelvic blood vessels become engorged with blood.

+ *For women:* The vagina lengthens and widens in preparation for the entry of the penis; the clitoris swells and enlarges; breasts swell and increase in sensitivity; the labia swell and separate; the vagina becomes lubricated. Vaginal lubrication (wetness) is one of the key indicators of physical arousal. In some cases, women may have medical difficulties that make lubrication difficult, such as menopause or hormone imbalance.

+ *For men:* The penis becomes erect; the scrotum thickens; the testes rise closer to the body. Erection of the penis is the key (and most obvious) indicator of sexual excitement.

Stage 3: Plateau

Once physical arousal is achieved and mental or physical stimulation continues, the plateau stage is achieved. The plateau stage involves a gradual build in sexual response to stimulation and is the high point of sexual excitement before orgasm. Reaching the plateau isn't a direct path to orgasm; it can be achieved, lost, and regained several times without the occurrence of orgasm.

Indications of the plateau stage. For both men and women there are several indicators that the plateau stage has been reached.

+ *For both sexes:* Breathing rate, heart rate, and blood pressure continue to increase; sexual flush deepens; muscle tension increases. Desire and physical arousal are at a high point here, and orgasm is within reach.

+ *For women:* The clitoris can become hypersensitive, lubrication increases, the areolae (the colored area) around the nipples become larger; the labia continue to swell; the uterus tips to stand high in the abdomen; the physical "orgasmic platform" develops, which means the walls of the vagina swell, causing the vagina to narrow and tighten.

+ *For men:* The head of the penis swells, pre-ejaculatory fluid is secreted and the testes rise closer to the body.

Stage 4: Orgasm

Orgasm occurs at the peak of the plateau stage. The sexual tension that has been building throughout the body releases and the chemicals called *endorphins* flood the bloodstream, creating a sense of well-being. People can achieve orgasm through mental stimulation and fantasy alone, but it results more commonly from direct physical stimulation or sexual intercourse (although many women report difficulty in achieving orgasm through vaginal intercourse alone). As stated earlier, women are capable of multiple orgasms (moving immediately from orgasm back into the plateau stage, then back to orgasm again), whereas men must pass through the resolution stage before another orgasm can be achieved.

Indications of orgasm. The intensity of orgasm can vary among individuals and can vary for an individual from one sexual experience to another. Orgasm may involve intense spasm and loss of awareness or only a sigh and subtle relaxation. It's different for everybody.

+ *For both sexes:* Heart rate, breathing, and blood pressure peak; sexual flush spreads over the body; there is a loss of muscle control (spasms).

+ *For women:* The uterus, vagina, anus, and muscles of the pelvic floor contract five to twelve times at 0.8-second intervals.

+ *For men:* Ejaculation occurs (contractions of the ejaculatory duct in the prostate gland cause semen to be ejected through the urethra and penis); the urethra, anus, and muscles of the pelvic floor contract three to six times at 0.8-second intervals.

Stage 5: Resolution

Resolution follows orgasm. Muscles relax, and the body returns to its pre-excitement state. Immediately following orgasm, men experience a *refractory period*, during which they can't have an erection. Women experience no refractory period. They can enter the resolution stage or return to the excitement or plateau stage immediately following orgasm.

Indications of resolution. There are various indicators of resolution for both men and women.

+ *For both sexes:* Heart rate and blood pressure dip below normal, then return quickly to normal; the whole body (including the palms of hands and soles of feet) sweats; there is a loss of muscle tension, increased relaxation, and drowsiness.

+ *For women:* Blood vessels dilate to drain the pelvic tissues and decrease engorgement; the breasts and areolae decrease in size; nipples lose their erection; the clitoris resumes its prearousal position and shrinks slightly; the labia return to normal size and position; the vagina relaxes; the cervix opens to help semen travel up into the uterus (closing twenty to thirty minutes after orgasm); the uterus lowers into the upper vagina.

+ *For men:* Nipples lose their erection; the penis lightens in color and becomes softer and smaller; the scrotum relaxes; the testes drop farther away from the body. Depending on a number of factors (including age), the resolution period in men may last anywhere from five minutes to twenty-four hours or more.

Consider yourself now armed with the fundamentals of human sexuality. Again, there are hundreds of books, articles, and websites that go into greater detail, such as *Intended for Pleasure* by Ed and Gaye Wheat and *When Two Become One* by Christopher and Rachel McCluskey. Too many men *think* about sex all the time while *knowing* very little about the basics. It's difficult for such men to become great lovers. If you approach the great mystery of sex equipped with knowledge, it will make trying to solve the mystery all the more enjoyable for you and your wife.

5

Knowing
the Dangers

Therefore, since we are surrounded by such a great cloud of
witnesses, let us throw off everything that hinders and the
sin that so easily entangles, and let us run with perseverance
the race marked out for us.

Hebrews 12:1 NIV

Bill was a forty-two-year-old associate pastor and married father
of three. When he called to make a therapy appointment, he
said he was having "marriage problems" and "just wanted an outsider's
perspective."

Bill said that he and his wife of sixteen years, Anna, weren't making love
as much as they once had. After several pointed questions, Bill confided
that he was the one who no longer had the drive for lovemaking.

Anna and Bill once enjoyed a rich love life. They had sex two or three times per week, and each of them felt satisfied. He and Anna were "soul mates," always able to connect on a deep physical and emotional level. But things had changed.

Two years ago Bill's church fired him over allegations that he was having an affair with the director of Christian education, a younger single woman. While Bill denied the affair, he admitted to having a relationship that lacked appropriate boundaries. Following this humiliating dismissal, Bill was unemployed for eight months. During this time, Bill used the Internet to research new ministry positions. With Anna and the kids out of the house most of the day, he succumbed to the temptation to explore Internet porn. He was instantly hooked. The pull to sexy, forbidden images was powerful. He masturbated multiple times per day, relishing the temporary escape into fantasy as a welcomed departure from his miserable reality. While his shame increased and self-esteem shrank, his once passionate relationship with his wife dwindled and died. With several hours of his day devoted to the world of Internet porn, he was neither physically nor emotionally capable of sexual intimacy with Anna.

In spite of his tainted résumé and daily diversions, Bill secured a position as associate pastor at a local church. Though his Internet experiences had decreased, he still found himself with very little desire to make love with Anna. She hadn't said much about it when he was unemployed, because she thought it was the result of his being fired. But now Bill didn't have the unemployment excuse. He wasn't interested in sex with Anna, and this worried him. Would she leave him? Would she find out about the porn? What would happen to their kids?

I asked Bill what he thought the problem was. His first thought was that the problem was spiritual. He knew that God disapproved of his Internet escapades, and perhaps he was being punished. Next he theorized that the problem was physical. He wasn't eighteen anymore and, as a smoker, he had heard of the negative impact nicotine has on potency.

Then there was Bill's family history. His parents divorced when his father had an affair. Though Bill didn't sleep with the woman at his former church, he thought about her frequently and began to wonder if adultery ran in the family. The men in his bloodline suffered from wanderlust, so perhaps his relationship with Anna had simply run its course.

Bill hated himself more during those eight months when he was unemployed than at any other time in his life. He had even had thoughts of suicide. His self-esteem was so low that he thought Anna would have sex with him only out of pity. Surely she wouldn't desire a man like him.

Bill's problems demonstrate how complex sexuality can be. Obstacles to healthy sex come in all shapes and sizes, and no one is immune.

Obstacles to Great Sex

Many men have a story that is similar to Bill's. Unfortunately, 31 percent of men (and 43 percent of women) will experience sexual dysfunction at some point in their life.[1] The good news is that most of these problems are easily treated with medical or psychological treatment. The following are the most common barriers to a healthy sex life.

Misinformation. Too many men lack a clear understanding of sexual procedures and their own sexuality. Ever hear the one about the man who thought it was okay to reuse a condom if he turned it inside out? I've known men who question their sexuality because they don't feel turned on by every woman they see. Men hold false beliefs on everything from birth control to sexual positions to the female sex drive. Too many have relied on "common sense" and locker-room talk for guidance. Jokes and pornography are lame educational resources, especially when there are books, websites, seminars, physicians, and counselors at your fingertips.

The past. You may have some dark moments in your sexual history. Whether they result from harmless show-and-tell, awkward teenage fumbling, or full-on sexual abuse, the past continues to haunt many men.

Their past imprisons them and makes them feel destined to fail. They carry their shame like a millstone around their neck, and if they don't talk about it, learn from it, and let it go, the weight gets heavier over time. Pastors, counselors, men's groups, and good friends are there to help us understand, accept, and heal our sexual wounds.

Poor role models. Our first example of adult male sexuality was our father. Not every man's father was a great lover. One man told me that he thought his parents were happily married but never saw them kiss or hold hands. Other men witnessed abuse and power struggles between their parents. It is not true that we inevitably become our father, but for harmful patterns to be avoided, we must make a conscious effort to choose another path.

Pornography. In the 1980s a senate judiciary committee found that adult bookstores in the United States outnumber McDonald's three to one. There are more than sixty-two million adult websites fueling a thirteen-billion-dollar industry.[2] Type almost any benign word into a search engine, and you're bound to come across a few adult websites. Men no longer need to seek out porn—it finds us.

The perils of pornography are well known and well documented. In addition to the clear scriptural admonishments against lust and coveting your neighbor's wife, pornography ruins intimacy within marriage. When a man seeks out sexual gratification via a fantasy connection with a fantasy woman, the marriage pays the price.

Addictions. We tend to think of chemicals when it comes to addiction. Certainly alcohol, tobacco, and other drugs form a substantial physical and emotional barrier to true intimacy. But addictions can be anything that enables us to detach from our everyday life. Gambling, video games, work, television, the Internet, sports, electronics, porn, numerous "harmless" hobbies, fitness, and even church can become addictions. Some men will conquer one addiction only to replace it with another. The Lord insists on being the only God in our lives. When we serve him first, we come to understand the importance of our marriage and the destructive nature of addictions.

Exhaustion. Making love is a workout. A sixty-hour workweek with a poor diet and no exercise is a recipe for a shrinking libido. Often, men who spend most of their twenty-four-hour day either at work or at social events don't have anything left for their marriage. While most men talk about the financial necessity of working all the time, some actually stay at work to avoid being home with their family. No wonder there aren't any sparks in the bedroom!

Body shame. A 1997 *Psychology Today* survey found that 43 percent of men are dissatisfied with their appearance. Thinning hair, beer bellies, poor muscle tone, and inadequate penis size were among their chief complaints. Sex requires a man to show up physically, and if he's feeling bad about his body, problems are inevitable.

Communication problems. On average, women speak ten thousand words per day, and men speak five thousand. This can be a problem for effective communication. Frequently a man comes to therapy and complains that his wife doesn't perform the way he'd like in the bedroom. Of course, he hasn't said anything to *her* about it. Men feel they don't have the words to explain what they want. They're afraid they'll hurt their wife's feelings or be rejected. Their silence leads to frustration, boredom, and even resentment toward their wife.

Sexual Disorders

Beyond the typical obstacles to great sex already discussed, there are certain sexual disorders. These are significant issues with biological or psychological roots requiring professional attention. If you suffer from any of the disorders discussed below, consult your physician or urologist and perhaps an experienced psychotherapist. Nearly one-third of all men suffer from a sexual disorder at some point during their lifetime. Treatment is readily available and often successful. There's no shame in having the problem; the shame is that many men don't seek help.

In the desire stage of the sexual response cycle, some men and women suffer from *hypoactive sexual desire disorder*. People with this problem experience a deficiency or absence of desire for sexual activity or even fantasy. These individuals rarely initiate sex, and when their partner initiates, they either reject the invitation or grudgingly comply. This is not simply a mismatch of sex drives, which occurs in many relationships, but a noticeable absence of sexual desire.

Sexual aversion disorder is an extreme aversion to all sexual contact. People suffering from this disorder report feeling anxious, fearful, or disgusted when the opportunity for sex arises. For some, this aversion is about particular aspects of sex (for example, bodily fluids or smells), while others are repulsed by sex in general.

Arousal disorders make up the next category, and they include *female sexual arousal disorder* and *male erectile disorder*. The female version is an inability to achieve or maintain adequate lubrication and swelling during sex. Without lubrication and swelling of the vaginal tissues, intercourse becomes painful or impossible.

Even if you don't have it, you've certainly heard of *erectile disorder*. You probably get a dozen emails per day selling prescriptions or herbal supplements to treat it. Erectile disorder is an inability to maintain an erection. Some decline in erectile function is natural as testosterone decreases with age, but erectile disorder is a much more severe problem than that.

Next are the orgasmic disorders. *Female and male orgasmic disorders* are the absence of orgasm following normal sexual desire and excitement. People who suffer from this disorder report feeling aroused at the onset of intercourse, but then the sex act becomes more of a chore than a pleasure.

Premature ejaculation is an orgasmic disorder that will afflict 27 percent of men in their lifetime. It is described as orgasm and ejaculation with minimal sexual stimulation before or shortly after penetration. One client described himself as a "two-pump chump" when divulging this problem. While it's normal for young men or men with a new sexual partner to ejaculate prematurely, consistent premature ejaculation indicates a disorder requiring treatment.

Finally, there are the *sexual pain disorders*. Both men and women can suffer from *dyspareunia*—genital pain experienced before, during, or after intercourse. Women may also suffer from *vaginismus*, which is a painful spasmodic contraction of the vaginal muscles when penetration with a finger, penis, or other object is attempted. Vaginismus is often mistaken for frigidity, but it is a sexual disorder that responds well to proper treatment.

Keeping Problems from Developing

As you see, there are a number of potential obstacles to great sex. But as one of the world's greatest lovers, you're working to free yourself from both shame and dysfunction. If you suffer from one of the problems described above, seek professional help from a physician or a sex therapist. If you don't suffer from any of these problems, guard against developing them with the following practices:

- *Take care of your body.* Drug abuse, alcohol abuse, smoking, a steady diet of fast food, laziness, and/or inadequate sleep can increase the likelihood of sexual problems. Take care of the ol' temple if you want the energy, stamina, and self-esteem for a mind-blowing sex life. See your physician at the first sign of sexual dysfunction. Hormones, circulatory problems, glandular issues, diet, depression, anxiety, and sleep deprivation can have serious sexual side effects. Great sex starts with the heart and soul, but it's the body that delivers the message. Get it in top condition.

- *Take care of your mind.* I'll bet you spend as much time on at least one hobby (model trains, downloading music, building one of those boats in a bottle) as you do on your relationship. Take a risk and make your relationship your top hobby for three months. Read

books, consult experts, and attend workshops. Form a men's group
to talk about tough marital issues and give one another feedback
and support. Journal a daily log of your marriage. Write down the
fantasies you have about your wife. They say the brain is the largest
sexual organ—stimulate it with positive, creative messages about
sex, intimacy, and romance.

* *Take care of your soul.* As we said earlier, a man who keeps God
  first in his life is on the way to being a great lover. Spend time
  daily in prayer. Commit Hebrews 12:1–2 to memory. If you have
  experienced spiritual shame (described earlier in this chapter) or
  misinformation, then continue to seek guidance and healing through
  praying, reading the Bible, talking with your pastor, confessing your
  sins, making restitution, and tithing. Find fellowship with other
  men to talk about marriage and just to enjoy guy time.

* *Take care of your emotions.* Many sexual problems have roots in
  painful past experiences. Plenty of men, especially those who
  grew up in "boys don't cry" environments, are emotionally con-
  stipated. Researchers found that men and women feel emotion to
  the same degree, but women express their emotions, while most
  men inhibit them.[3] You may have prided yourself on controlling
  your emotions through the years, but now you find yourself with
  a few problems. As shrinks, we're biased, but maybe therapy is
  something to consider. If not, at least find a solid mentor or a
  group of friends.

* *Take care of your relationship.* Last and definitely not least, your
  relationship deserves all the time and effort you can give. Your wife
  is not just a roommate or sex partner; she's your partner in life. Take
  risks with her that you never dared to take before, such as talking
  about emotions, asking her why she loves you, telling her why you
  love her, and telling her a sexual fantasy you have. Let yourself cry
  with her. Recommit yourself to sharing life with her. That's what
  you promised at the altar, right?

We won't leave you hanging regarding Pastor Bill. Through the course of therapy, he got in touch with the anger he felt toward his philandering dad—an anger that freed him to see himself as a man who didn't need to walk in his dad's footsteps. He opened up to Anna, confessing his pornography struggles as well as his temptations toward the woman at his previous church. He let her know the things about their marriage that were frustrating and how terrified he was that she might leave when she found out what a loser he was. While upset, his wife was pleased finally to hear the truth, and she made a commitment to support him. Bill put aside his distracting addictions and reconnected with Anna. Not every day is a walk in the park for Bill. He still wrestles with low self-esteem, but he no longer pushes Anna away. With the help of his wife, close friends, therapist, and his *only* God, Jesus Christ, Bill no longer fights his battles alone.

6

Knowing Who
You Are

At the beginning of creation God "made them male and female." "For this reason a man will leave his father and mother and be united to his wife, and the two will become one flesh." So they are no longer two, but one. Therefore what God has joined together, let man not separate.

Mark 10:6–9 NIV

The most vital, passionate, intimate marriages are experienced by two people who know who they are as individuals and who have a deep desire to share their self with their partner. Intimacy is not about being dependent on one another or completely independent. It involves true *interdependence*: two people coming together to support and love each other deeply while still maintaining their own identity.

Think back to the beginning of your relationship with your wife, when you first got serious. You couldn't keep your hands off each other. It didn't matter if you were in the car, in the movie theater, or in her parents' living room. Let's be honest—even in church. You were thinking about being with her, and she was thinking about being with you. School, work, friends, sleep—nothing else mattered.

Let's explore the circumstances for a moment. You had your life, and she had hers. You had your own place; so did she. You had different friends. You had a deep, rich history that was brand-new to her, and she had her own interesting past. You talked about all sorts of things, agreeing on some, disagreeing on others. You were different people with different lives, and that's part of what made your courtship tantalizing. You were crazy about each other. Her stories fascinated you, and you were eager to tell her yours. The two of you looked forward to all the incredible things you were going to experience together, especially sex. You were free to be yourself, and she was mesmerizing.

As your relationship progressed toward marriage, the two of you drew closer to one another and you shared more and more of your lives together. You may have found that you were willing to spend less time with your own friends, and she was too. Instead of "I," "me," and "mine," the language of the relationship changed to "we," "us," and "ours." Because of your love and desire to make each other happy, you occasionally put your own needs and wants on hold to accommodate her. These personal sacrifices are some of the most loving acts we do for one another.

The Problem with Accommodation

Over time, however, this accommodation can have its downside. Surrendering your own wants is not always best for the relationship. For example, it may not be a big deal for you to agree to spend your vacation with your mother-in-law this year, but spending every summer with her for the next forty years may cause some problems. As a couple, you face numerous situations that require each of you to state your honest opinion rather than to acquiesce. Issues such as where you'll live, how many children you'll have, and where you'll attend church require both of you to express your opinions. When you develop a habit of accommodating rather than stating your feelings, resentments build and the passion can start to fade.

Accommodation and diminished passion are normal in marriage, and many couples accept these patterns as facts of life. But you're reading this book because you hope there's something more to be achieved in your marriage and your sex life. Passion comes from taking the risk to be emotionally vulnerable in your relationship. Therefore we invite you and your wife to be open and honest with each other, to be who you really are, to rekindle the flames of your romance. When you hold back, you are cheating yourself of the joyful, passionate intimacy that keeps love alive and makes sparks fly in the bedroom. This active, alive, intimate, and honest connection is what we call a *vital marriage*, and it is possible only when a couple is willing to face their fears of vulnerability.

Humans thrive when they can be connected with others and maintain their own identity. Psychologist David Schnarch calls this *differentiation*, while John Eldredge speaks of maintaining the *mystery*. Call it what you will, preserving a vibrant self and fueling the desire to connect with your wife in a deeply passionate way prepare the way for intimate lovemaking.

Having your own identity isn't about becoming a selfish jerk or distancing yourself from your wife. It's about getting back in touch with the kind of relationship you had when you first dated, back when you were you and she was she, when you both spoke your mind because it was all you knew, back when you wanted each other so much it hurt.

Wisdom for a Vital Marriage

By now we hope that some thoughts are stirring about the importance of married partners maintaining their sense of self within the marriage. You may be starting to think about the ways in which you've let some of your own interests fade in the face of your coupledom. Intimacy exists when two people with a solid understanding of themselves come together to know and be known by each other. For this to happen, it is important to know your wants and feelings, talk about them, tolerate the disagreements, and grow to accept and appreciate your uniqueness.

Know Your Wants and Feelings

We have the following interaction quite often with the men who come to therapy. They rush to the office after a long day of work and tell us about everything they've done over the past week. When we ask them how they feel or what they want from today's session, we get a blank stare.

Most men aren't so great at identifying their feelings, yet it's a skill that can be developed. At first, this may seem like learning a foreign language, but with practice it won't seem forced to look within and identify how you feel. To do this, some people find it helpful to keep a journal, jot down notes, or set aside a few minutes each day (maybe on the drive to work or while in the shower) to focus on what's important. Some men get in touch with their feelings when they have quiet time with the Lord. Others find that a small-group Bible study or other fellowship time helps them connect to their feelings while connecting with others.

If you are to bring your whole self into your marital relationship, it is important to stay in touch with your wants and feelings. You need to know what is important to you—your values, beliefs, faith, goals, dreams, and fantasies. Then you can share them with your wife.

Need some help getting started? Try answering these questions, and remember, be honest with yourself.

What's the best part of my life today?

What area of my life needs the most work?

Who is God to me today?

What is the best/worst thing about being me?

If I were to meet someone like me, would I like him?

What was my best/worst day?

When I was a kid, who did I want to be as a grownup?

What is the best thing about my marriage?

What area of my marriage needs the most work?

What do I want?

How do I feel?

Most of the time men just need to slow down enough to let their wants and feelings catch up with them, to think about them. Make this slower time a priority for you. It could greatly enhance the quality of your marriage.

Sometimes, in spite of all the self-examination, some men still aren't clear about their role as husband and lover. This would be an occasion to draw on the "cloud of witnesses" mentioned in Hebrews 12:1. We have learned that Christians are called to imitate Christ, and we need to identify people in our lives today who do that and whom we can imitate—people like the heroes in Hebrews. Men need heroes. As kids, we pinned up posters of sports heroes; we strapped on capes and fantasized about being superheroes. We said things like: "My dad can beat up your dad." Today there are probably men in your life whom you admire for their social skills, their business acumen, or their unwavering faith. Why not have an intimacy hero?

I (RH) think of my high school Bible study leader. He has an incredible faith, a strong fellowship with other men, and a deeply satisfying relationship with his wife. When I first met him, he had three young kids, but he always maintained a ritual of one night per week and one week per year to spend only with his wife. They laugh, argue, debate, and genuinely like being with one another. Their three decades together have been unlike any I've seen. I can only hope my marriage follows their example. They are my intimacy heroes.

Because I know this couple, I can ask myself, in tough moments in my marriage, what they would do. I might even call them on the phone and discuss a problem with them. It's important to discover and use intimacy resources, people who model intimacy and can give you good advice. Don't reinvent the wheel when it comes to something as important as intimacy. Find mentors you respect and learn from them.

Be a Man of Your Word

Once you have a better idea of what you want and how you feel, it's time to speak up to your wife. It's time to communicate openly with her.

Chances are, your wife still has a stash of your old love letters kept in a safe place. During the earliest days of your relationship, you spoke and wrote expressions of your love that were incredibly intimate and vulnerable. Why do you now hesitate to verbalize your feelings? Because you got comfortable, or you figured she knew how you felt and saying it again would be redundant. More to the point, however, the love notes became rare because in marriage you are more vulnerable and expressing feelings at that deep level is scary. True, it might be uncomfortable, but if better lovemaking comes from deeper intimacy and greater vulnerability, that's exactly where you need to go. If you've explored your feelings about your marriage and found love, let her know—frequently.

But open, intimate communication isn't just about loving feelings. In *Wild at Heart* John Eldredge challenges men to "let people feel the weight of who you are, and let them deal with it."[1] Telling your wife your feelings about spending each summer with her mother might seem like a difficult discussion, but the difficulty pales in comparison to the anguish you'll feel during years of resentment if you don't speak up. Authentic intimacy means saying the unpopular truths when necessary, even if you believe it will hurt. She might not like hearing your wants and feelings, but she'll respect your honesty. She'll also feel respected by you because you trusted her to hear and deal with something difficult.

Regardless of whether the news is good or bad, it's vitally important to maintain open communication in your marriage. It's too easy to meander through life going from one minicrisis or period of doldrums to the next, completely out of touch with each other. Taking the time to step back and observe the relationship once in a while can provide a forum for discussing fresh hurts, uncovering hidden needs, and celebrating successes.

We suggest having a regular "State of the Union Address." Every couple of weeks, when you and your wife are enjoying a peaceful moment, start talking about the state of your union. Take turns going first, and talk about what seems to be working and what needs attention. Level with each other; don't hold back. Talk about how you feel, what you want, and what you appreciate. Discuss how you're doing as an individual and how you think the relationship is growing. Your wife will be flattered that you're initiating this relationship status report, and your intimacy will deepen as a result.

We're calling you to be a man of your word. On your wedding day, in front of God, family, friends, and your spouse, you uttered your vows. At that point, at the pinnacle of sacred moments in your life, you uttered words that were keys to essential intimacy.

Whether you wrote your own vows or used the old standards, your words summed up how you intended to relate to your wife from that day forward. "I . . . take you . . . To have and to hold. . . . In sickness and in health. . . . Honor, cherish. . . . Love."

Those were not just quaint words spoken lightly on your way to the honeymoon. You meant them in the moment and you committed to them for life. Be a man of your word. Live that oath every day. If you've forgotten your vows, dust off the wedding album or throw in the video and relive them. Commit them to memory. The self that spoke those words on your wedding day intended for you to live those vows today.

Love Your Disagreements

Somewhere in history, a snake-oil salesman sold us on the idea that happy couples agree on everything. This notion has contributed to millions of couples trying and failing to reach this impossible goal, ending up in misery. Not only is perfect agreement impossible, it's not even desirable.

Imagine this: your wife comes home and tells you that she'd really like to turn the TV room into a cat hotel where people around town can board their cats while they're on vacation.

At this point, you have three choices: accommodate, react, or explore. If you choose to accommodate, then say good-bye to the new HD plasma television. To maintain "harmony" and "keep the peace," you will go along with your wife's idea, keep your mouth shut, and try to learn to love the smell of cat pee. The snake-oil man taught you well. You are the picture of compliance, a truly nice guy. Inside, however, you will be a seething cauldron of self-loathing bitterness. You've thrown away all sense of self for the sake of "harmony." By the way, you won't be able to keep smiling forever. Your resentment will burn a hole in your stomach, and you'll find ways—direct or indirect—to let your wife know how angry you are.

On hearing your wife's idea, the majority of you would go into react mode. "Are you out of your mind?" you'd yell. You would quash her dream and get into a big argument, then go to bed mad at each other. You would think your wife's a nut for suggesting such a thing, and she'd think you're a jerk for not hearing her out. Nice work!

Men and women solve problems differently. Most men need to think things through, then speak their conclusion, while women typically need to talk through their decision-making process. More often than not, women think out loud. When your wife came through the door with her cat hotel idea, chances are she just wanted to toss it out because she thought it was an interesting idea at the time. You, on the other hand, assumed she was wired more like you, that she had mulled the idea over for a day and a half, had a floor plan and marketing strategy in mind, and was springing it on you. You explode with "Over my dead body!" as if she's got a litter of kittens in her purse.

For many men, disagreements activate a primal "fight or flight" response. Rather than respond rationally, men react and suddenly want to conquer the foe. In the case of your marriage, your "foe" is actually your greatest ally, your wife; and "winning" actually results in losing closeness. Most arguments boil down to one decision—either you can win or you stay in relationship. It is best for you to take a moment to step back and regain your senses before reacting with poor judgment that produces miserable consequences. It's not wise to make important relationship decisions while in the eye of the storm. Collect yourself first.

"So, tell me about this idea," you might say calmly. "How did you come up with it?" You could spend quite awhile exploring the idea, curious about her reasoning. After hearing her out, you would then present your own ideas, dissimilar as they might be. You would explain why you have these thoughts and feelings. You might choose to pray together to seek God's guidance as you make your decision. After a bit of loving dialogue and reflection, you would decide what to do with the TV room. Deciding in this way won't deprive you of the opportunity to learn from each other's differences.

Your differences don't have to be a threat. In fact, they're a blessing. Intimate couples who are in a vital marriage love the way their spouses view the world with eyes that are different from theirs. Each disagreement that a couple has provides an opportunity to learn, grow, and see the world from a different perspective.

Men and women are wired differently and will forever remain mysterious to one another. This is something to be cherished not feared.

Appreciate Your Uniqueness

What is different about you? What sets you apart from your wife and from other people? What opinions, interests, and experiences in your life make you unique? All too often, men feel as though marriage is meant to squelch characteristics that don't conform to their wife's or society's or their church's vision of marriage. They set down the guitar, cut their hair, quit the poker night, and stop having unique interests. Consider the idea that your distinctive interests may be what drew your wife to you in the first place. Think about her too. What was unique about her?

The two of you were drawn together because you were interested in something intriguing about each other, something different from any other person in the world. Remember?

Marriage is no time to lose your self. On the contrary, it's the best time to grow. As two become one in the Lord, unique talents, gifts, and special qualities should be allowed to flourish. How can you help rekindle or nurture her distinctive qualities? How can she help you?

Make it your goal to learn about and encourage your wife in her uniqueness. Support her and encourage her in her endeavors without envy or possessiveness. And share with her your uniqueness, and let her know how she can support you.

How well do you know your wife—her routines, her goals, and her memories? Try answering the following questions, then run your answers by her. You might be surprised by what you learn.

What is your wife's favorite television show? Of all time?

What are your wife's greatest goals?

What stresses your wife out?

What is your wife's favorite meal?

What is your wife's favorite Scripture?

What is your wife's fondest childhood memory?

What is your wife's idea of a perfect day?

What is your wife's greatest fear?

What does a typical day involve for your wife?

What turns your wife on sexually?

What would your wife want you to change about yourself?

What are your wife's hobbies?

What does your wife wish you knew about sex?

Intimacy: A Lifetime Pursuit

At the beginning of this chapter, we talked about how important it is to be free to be yourself. In a marriage filled with *us* and *we*, it can be difficult to get back in touch with *I*. But true intimacy can develop only between two intact selves, people who know who they are as individuals.

The quest for intimacy can be a lifelong journey of increasing depth and challenge. That's what makes marriage so incredible. If you so choose, it can offer an endless amount of growth and exploration. Only your fears stand in the way. It takes teamwork, communication, patience, and sweat to overcome an obstacle as huge as fear. But remember, you came together because you wanted all of her to accompany all of you into the uncertain future.

7

Knowing How
to Be Alone

Times of separation can present challenges for intimacy and sexuality. When you or your wife are away on a trip, working long hours, preoccupied with something urgent, or ill, it can create physical and/or emotional distance that impedes intimacy. But your sexuality doesn't go away when your wife isn't there. You'll still get horny. In fact (and it hurts to tell you this), you'll be more horny.[1] If you're away from your wife for more than a day or two, there's a chance your testosterone levels will rise, making you more of a heat-seeking missile than you already are.

But don't despair. In this chapter, we'll look at some ways to manage sexual desire, and we'll see that dealing with sexual arousal is the *easy* part of separation. The hard part—the part that really determines how well you handle being alone—is maintaining something we call *attachment*.

Attachment

Attachment is the bedrock of intimacy. It's the emotional bond we have with another person. More than just commitment, it's an enduring feeling of connection.

The best way to explain this is to describe a developmental phenomenon called *object permanence*. Object permanence means knowing something is there even when you can't see it. Until a baby is about eight months old, he or she lacks object permanence. For example, if an infant is watching a ball roll across the floor, and then it rolls behind the couch where he can't see it, the baby will think the ball has vanished. The child doesn't understand that the ball is still there, only out of sight. This is one of the reasons babies giggle at the game of peekaboo. Cover up your face in front of an infant, and it seems to the baby as if your face has disappeared. Then uncover it and make a funny noise and *presto!* you've just performed a magic trick. Once the baby develops object permanence, peekaboo is no longer amusing, unless the kid just gets a kick out of watching Dad act goofy.

Attachment is *emotional* object permanence in relationships. A man with a secure sense of attachment will still feel connected to his wife even when she's not there. A man without attachment can have an array of difficulties when separated from his wife. Some men grow anxious or depressed, while others have difficulty remaining faithful. Some men experience lower self-esteem away from their wife's attention. Some might even struggle with jealousy and paranoia, convinced that other men will lure their wife away. Still other men might feel more relaxed when their wife is away, because they have difficulty with intimacy and want to avoid feelings of attachment.

Up to this point, we've talked a lot about developing a strong, masculine identity separate from your wife and parents. That's crucial. There's another step, however, for a man to take if he is to have a healthy marriage. He needs a strong, stable attachment with his wife. He needs an emotional bond with her that he integrates into his identity. This means that, at any place or time, he has a sense of being in relationship with his wife. He may miss her and ache to see her, and he'll have no doubt that the relationship is still strong. He has *internalized* the relationship so it feels like part of who he is.

Being alone is easier with a strong sense of attachment. It affects everything, including how you handle sexual temptation. A man who feels attached to his wife will:

+ miss his wife when separated from her without becoming anxious
+ be able to enjoy other friends and interests without feeling as though he's doing something wrong or betraying his marriage
+ see an attractive woman without being overcome by desire and think, *I appreciate that* rather than *I need to have that*, because he's satisfied with the attachment he feels to his wife
+ be able to tolerate disagreements and disappointments in marriage without feeling the urge to either avoid or control his wife
+ experience a reunion with his wife as joyful and relaxed rather than awkward, anxious, or irritating
+ have strong bonds with other men that do not interfere with feelings of connection with his wife, and vice versa!
+ enjoy his own company when he is alone
+ have incredible sex with his wife but still feel close to her without it

Now these are the qualities of a *very* strong attachment. If a couple of these are lacking or occasionally problematic, don't worry. If most of these ring true, chances are you have a solid attachment to your wife and being separated from her isn't too challenging. However, if these qualities aren't familiar and represent areas of struggle, your relationship needs some work.

Developing Attachment

We wish we could give you a simple five-step plan for developing a strong attachment to your wife, but unfortunately, it's not that easy. Secure emotional attachment is related to a variety of factors, the most potent being childhood experiences with your family. Problems with attachment don't change overnight. However, there's a lot you can do to develop the type of emotional connection that will make your marriage better and your time away from your wife much easier.

The Attachment Expert

God is the attachment expert. He knows more about love and intimacy than any of us, because he created love and intimacy. Start by asking God to enter into your relationship and make it stronger. And don't just ask once. Stay in constant contact with God, praying daily for his intervention. Being intentional about seeking God through your marriage will do more than anything else to begin building a strong attachment.

The Proper Attachment

Men are to love and respect their wives, not fear or worship them. Some men fear their wives, but you'd never know it because they express this fear as anger and resentment. Disagreements, denials, and disappointments make them furious. If their wives remind them to take out the trash or point out a mistake, they become furious and think they're nags. These men need to cool their jets and stop making their wives so powerful.

So your wife disagrees with you or gets impatient sometimes? *So what?* Her feelings are important, but you don't have to give her so much power and get upset whenever she's upset. If you respect and love her, you'll be able to listen to her without feeling like you're in trouble or injured every time she reminds you to put the toilet seat down.

Men who fear their wives relish being away from them, whether it's a business trip or hiding out in the garage. Men who love and respect their wives can be around them even when things aren't pleasant. This doesn't mean that you shouldn't have some time away—everybody needs to be alone or with other friends sometimes; but you won't feel a need to escape just because she's in a bad mood. In other words, you won't take it personally.

An Important Obstacle to Attachment

When a man or a couple comes to therapy due to difficulties in attachment, usually it takes only a few questions about their past to find out where the problems started. The way a man's parents connected with him and the way they connected with each other have tremendous impact on their child's capacity for attachment. The best way to get at this is with the help of a counselor. Counseling for couples and marriage enrichment seminars are also great ways to begin fostering more intimacy and attachment. And don't think your marriage has to be on the rocks before you begin exploring the effects of your past. Too often, couples seek help only after tremendous damage has been done. The sooner you start exploring hidden obstacles to attachment, the better your marriage will be.

Sexual Temptation

Even with a solid attachment to his wife, a man can't avoid sexual temptation. Our culture bombards us with sexual images that make it inevitable. When you're alone, this temptation becomes more powerful.

There are about a hundred different behavioral strategies for avoiding and overcoming sexual temptation, and there are a lot of excellent resources. For example, if you're sitting at your computer and feel tempted to look at Internet porn, simply do a search on something like "overcoming Internet pornography." You'll find dozens of websites that give you immediate ways to cope with temptation.

Ultimately, however, you'll want to get beyond relying on behavioral strategies alone. The best resistance comes from your heart and your character rather than from dropping and doing twenty push-ups every time you see a sexy woman. As we've just discussed, feeling a strong sense of attachment to your wife will increase your resistance to sexual temptation. Your connection with her makes things like pornography, strip clubs, and flirting with a co-worker less attractive.

Even with a strong attachment, though, behavioral strategies may sometimes be necessary. When you stay in a hotel room alone, you may need to block out the "adult" channels. If you're alone in front of a computer a lot, you may need an accountability partner or an Internet service provider that won't access pornographic sites. We all need a little extra help to resist the continual siege of temptation and elicit images. But we want to emphasize that your greatest strength in fighting sexual temptation comes from your heart and your character.

Remember Who You Are

The discovery that American soldiers tortured Iraqi prisoners following the Iraq War touched off heated debate in Washington, D.C. There was disagreement about how far we should go in interrogating a prisoner of war. Many argued that, since the enemy did horrible things to our soldiers, Americans were justified in using the same methods. Senator John McCain, however, disagreed. He said that torture was wrong not because it wasn't "fair," but because it didn't reflect American ideals and principles. He said: "We are different and better than our enemies. . . . we fight for an idea, not a tribe, not a land, not a king, not a twisted interpretation of an ancient religion, but for an idea that all men are created equal and endowed by their Creator with inalienable rights."[2] In other words, it's about "us" not "them." McCain argued that we are "better" than torture and shouldn't succumb to the temptation to behave like our enemies. Likewise, you are "better" than sexual temptation.

The next time you find yourself bombarded by tempting thoughts, pause for a moment and think about *who you are*. Attempt to rise above the immediate temptation and think about the kind of man you are.

What do you believe in? What's important to you? Who is important to you? Spend time meditating on these questions, and you'll probably have difficulty seeing yourself as someone who gives in to sexual temptation. You'll realize that you're "better" than pornography and adultery. You're not the kind of man who does that. Even if you've had weak moments before, they don't define you.

It may be that another need is rearing its head and you're trying to squelch it with porn. Ask yourself, *How do I feel? What am I really looking for?* This can redirect your thoughts toward what you really need, whether it's a little exercise or a new sense of purpose and direction. Answering these questions will bring a dose of reality to your fantasy world. And it can take all the fun out of porn and other forms of temptation.

Thinking about who you are is even more effective than thinking about the pain that your succumbing to temptation will cause your wife. It's important to acknowledge your wife's pain, but it's not the best motivator. Though the idea of hurting your wife should be a strong deterrent, the thing that will help you overcome sexual temptation in the long run is a sense that you're not the kind of man who does that, regardless of whether your wife knows about it. Pride is a far better motivator than guilt.

Remember Whose You Are

The father and son story of *The Lion King* teaches a good lesson about knowing who you are and *whose* you are. After a rival kills off Mufasa, the lion king, his son, Simba, flees into exile. Alone and without purpose, Simba gives up on being a king and spends his time eating grubs with a meerkat and a warthog. Then, when he rediscovers who he is, everything changes. While looking into a pool of water, he sees his father's reflection in his own. Mufasa's ghost says, "Simba, you have forgotten me. You have forgotten who you are and so have forgotten me. Look inside yourself, Simba. You are more than what you have become. Remember who you are. You are my son and the one true king."

Your heavenly Father says the same to you. Jesus said, "On that day you will realize that I am in my Father, and you are in me, and I am in you" (John 14:20 NIV). Every time you begin to pray the Lord's Prayer, you speak to your Father as a son. Your Father is the real Lion King, the Lion of Judah. He gives you purpose, identity, and a kingdom to build.

Meditating on your relationship with God will go a long way toward helping you defeat temptation. Whether it's through prayer, praise, or reading the Bible or another spiritual book, reconnecting with God will make whatever is tempting you less attractive. It will reconnect you to your Lord, King, Savior, and Father. It will remind you that God has better things in mind for you than a cheap sexual release.

Ideally, remembering God won't help just because it makes you feel guilty. Remember, guilt is a poor motivator for the long term. But if you remember that God loves you intimately and created you for his special purpose and joy, it can make you feel "above" sexual temptation. It can make you feel like you deserve more. You deserve great sex with someone who loves you and is committed to you. Turning toward God can allow you to transcend your sex drive and connect to something greater.

And God is eager to help. Sexual temptation is common and powerful—God knows that. He understands those desires that drive you crazy and make you leave teeth marks in your pen. God is not some distant judge, waiting to see if you pass a test. He wants to *help* you pass the test. You can even think of it as cheating! Imagine Satan as a mean grade-school teacher giving you an exam that seems impossible. Then God sits down next to you and says, "Don't worry. We're going to do this together, and I happen to know all the answers." It won't always feel that way, but you can rest in this: "No temptation has seized you except what is common to man. And God is faithful; he will not let you be tempted beyond what you can bear. But when you are tempted, he will also provide a way out so you can stand up under it" (1 Cor. 10:13 NIV). Whether you feel it or not, God is ready to walk through your trials with you.

Remember Your Purpose

Restraint alone is a lousy way to overcome any form of temptation. In fact, it will make matters worse. Most men react to temptation by thinking, *I shouldn't do it. I can't do it no matter what! I have to be strong!* We call this "white knuckling," and it usually guarantees that you'll do that thing you don't want to do. In telling yourself repeatedly *not* to do something, you end up obsessing about the very thing you don't want to do. You become preoccupied with what you're trying to avoid. This is one of the reasons most diets fail. If you obsess over what you eat, you spend a lot of time thinking about what you *can't* eat. That makes you hungry. The same thing applies to sexual temptation.

As we said earlier, you have to redirect your thoughts and emotions when faced with sexual temptation. You need something more important and exciting to think about or do. Focusing on your purpose and passions is an excellent way to redirect your thoughts. God has something important for you to do, my friend, and it will be much more gratifying than satisfying the sexual impulse that's driving you nuts. Redirect your energy toward that important goal. It may be time for you to start an exercise program or maybe God has been calling you to develop a passion for something that you've ignored for too long. Above all, you must turn your thoughts toward ideas and goals that are more meaningful than the immediate temptation.

One of the reasons some men have difficulty being alone is that their lives lack passion and adventure. Nothing excites, intrigues, or compels them. This creates what seminal psychologist Viktor Frankl calls an *existential vacuum*.[3] It can be filled only with a sense of meaning, purpose, and passion. If a man lacks these things, he'll try to fill the existential vacuum with idle distraction, making money, or more immediate gratifications, such as food, alcohol, and sex. Such a man feels this existential vacuum most acutely when alone. If his wife isn't there to distract him, he'll feel bored, restless, or even anxious.

God created you to be passionate about something. God created you with a mission and purpose in mind. If you have no idea what that is, then figuring it out can become your purpose for now. Regardless, refocusing on something more important will make sexual temptation feel petty and powerless compared to that "great thing" God wants you to do. Time alone can become an opportunity for growth and adventure instead of an occasion for temptation and frustration.

But remember not to pour *all* your energy into something other than your marriage. If you devote too much passion to other pursuits, regardless of how noble they may be, you'll have less time and energy left for your wife. A strong man stores up some energy for his wife. When he's with her again and has the opportunity to release it, the reunion will be sweet.

PART THREE

Knowing
Love

8

Knowing How
to Love Her

Love is patient, love is kind. It does not envy, it does not boast,
it is not proud. It is not rude, it is not self-seeking, it is not easily
angered, it keeps no record of wrongs. Love does not delight
in evil but rejoices with the truth. It always protects, always
trusts, always hopes, always perseveres. Love never fails.

1 Corinthians 13:4–8 NIV

What Does a Woman Want?

For men to become great lovers, we need to look at the greatest lover
who ever lived: Jesus. Jesus's ministry could be summed up in one word:
with. God sent his Son to be *with* us here on earth, to share in our lives,
to be with us in our struggles, and to heal our suffering. Jesus was called
Immanuel: "God *with* us" (Matt. 1:23 NIV).

To love our wives as Christ loves us, we must learn to be *with* them
emotionally, spiritually, physically, and sexually. We got married to share

our lives with one another, a fact that is too easily forgotten. Work, arguments, kids, resentments, and temptations cloud this once clear intention. Men need to evaluate how much they are *with* their wife on a daily basis. Consider the following illustration from one of our favorite sermons.

In a dream a man saw images of heaven and hell. In hell he saw a long banquet table with an incredible spread of the best food he'd ever seen. The only catch was everyone had utensils that were four feet long. When the people sat down to eat, they tried to use their incredibly long forks to feed themselves and got nowhere. It was impossible for them to get any food in their mouths, so everyone went hungry.

In heaven the man saw the same scene—the long banquet table, the amazing feast, and the long utensils. But when the people sat down to eat, they used the long forks to reach across the table to feed the person across from them. They served each other, everyone enjoyed the meal, and no one went hungry.

Your marriage demands this kind of teamwork. Probably one of your marriage vows was to serve your wife ahead of yourself, and she committed to do the same for you. Ideally, you will be feeding each other an incredible banquet for the rest of your lives.

The verses from 1 Corinthians 13 at the beginning of the chapter may be familiar to you. There's even a good chance they were read at your wedding. Those words encapsulate God's perfect recipe for love. Read them again. Memorize them. They are all you need to know to love and *be with* your wife. Think we're kidding? As we worked on this chapter, we decided to practice what we preach. We asked our wives what makes them feel loved. They didn't use exactly the same words as Paul in 1 Corinthians, but the message was identical. The following eight points are their responses, with our commentary.

Empathy

Our wives said they feel loved when we empathize with them. They were firm on this point. When they're feeling bad about something, it makes them feel a lot better if we try to understand what's upsetting them and why. They feel important and cared for when we empathize.

You may have had a tough day today. You were stuck in traffic, your boss was a pain, and your favorite lunch spot was shut down by the health department. Days like this are draining, and all you want when you get home is a beer or soda and *SportsCenter*. Who can blame you?

But your wife had a tough day too. Her presentation at work was a disaster, she's fighting a cold, and her mother has been dishing it out extra thick lately. She's looking for her "beer and *SportsCenter*" too. But hers might look different from yours. Maybe her "cold drink" is a neck massage from you and her *SportsCenter* is a half hour of talking. Empathy entails taking the time to understand things from her perspective.

An interesting phenomenon happens in relationships. When you sacrifice your needs for your spouse, things get better. You feel good about being a good partner. Your spouse appreciates you and wants to return the favor. With your wife's help, your needs are met better than you expected. You might get a cold beer, *SportsCenter, and* a plate of nachos! You're feeding one another with those four-foot forks.

To love your wife, you will need to put her needs in front of yours. You need to put aside your selfish desires for a while and understand how she feels and what you can give her. This may take practice, because you may have spent years perfecting the art of selfishness. But when you do figure it out, you'll know the joy of being in partnership with a trusted companion.

Support

This one surprised us a little. Our wives said that they consider the little chores we do around the house some of the greatest acts of love.

Your wife wants to know that you value all she does and that you're willing to help out. This includes (but is not limited to) housework and child care. Sometimes it's important to pull your head out of your cell phone or palm pilot and appreciate her. Use some elbow grease and join in from time to time. Clean something; cook something; sweep something; walk a mile in her shoes.

Support extends beyond the home as well. Your wife may have career interests, hobbies, relationships, or dreams that extend outside your four walls. She may need your help with time, motivation, or working out the logistics to make her desires come true. We encourage you to develop an attitude of curiosity about her life beyond your relationship. You may learn something exciting about her that takes your relationship to the next level.

Patience

When our wives see our furrowed brow because we have to wait for them, they know we have grown impatient. They feel loved when we remain calm and try to understand.

Patience shows up in two ways. There's short-term patience and long-term patience. Short-term patience is toughest for most men. It's needed when your wife has said, "I'll be ready in ten minutes" an hour ago. Or "I'm just dropping by the shoe store," and she's in there for an hour. Guys hate to wait. We can buy a suit in ten minutes and a new car in thirty. Some women can take days to make up their mind.

If you're going to love your wife, you need to gain some perspective here. Going to a party has an entirely different meaning for the two of you. For your wife, it's important that she look her best. Shoes mean something very different too. She has to find just the right pair. If you're stuck waiting for her, try something new. Ask if you can help with her decision or preparation. You'll be joining the team, showing her that you care, and potentially speeding up the process (but don't count on it). At least you'll have a better understanding of why it takes her so long.

Long-term patience requires the same committed love on a larger scale. We all have goals and aspirations that seem forever lost to procrastination. Extend to your wife the same patience you'd like in return: pray for her, encourage her, and support her in a loving way. Refrain from nagging and nit-picking. Remember, love is patient and kind!

Conversation

Our wives mentioned that some of the moments they cherish most are the conversations we have together. They feel connected when we simply talk.

Like we said earlier, each day women say twice as many words as men. Men tend to think then speak, while women tend to think aloud. But women feel loved when their man shares his thoughts with her.

Married couples often come to therapy unaware of how far apart they've grown. They get this homework assignment in the first session: talk with each other for fifteen minutes each day. They're advised that discussing their schedules or musing about the weather doesn't count. They need to talk about themselves or their relationship. They leave the session saying, "Sure! No problem!" They return shocked at how difficult the assignment was for them. Learn how to talk with your wife, sharing your life and learning about hers. Make it a regular part of your day.

Surprises

According to our wives, surprises make them feel loved. The fact that we put time and effort into planning a surprise, no matter how big or small, lets them know we care about them.

Birthdays, Christmas, anniversaries, and other holidays give us many built-in opportunities to buy gifts and show appreciation, but surprises go further than this. A little sticky note with "I love you!" in her purse qualifies as a surprise. Buying her a book by her favorite author does too. How about a surprise candle-and-massage-oil night, or a scavenger hunt, concert tickets, takeout from her favorite restaurant, a love poem, a spontaneous sexual interlude, washing her car, or a romantic weekend getaway? The sky's the limit. Just make sure the surprise isn't outside her comfort zone, or it could backfire.

The idea behind this is simple: we all want to know that our spouse loves us and thinks about us when we're not sitting right in front of her.

Assure your wife of this by making or planning loving gestures toward her when you're away from her. She's a top priority to you, and a surprise will communicate this.

Play

Our wives talked about a phenomenon that occurs on the third day of a weeklong vacation. We relax and start to have fun. We joke around, talk in silly voices (that we'd never let our guy friends hear), laugh, tease, and lighten up. When we lose our businesslike demeanor and play around, our wives feel loved.

When we enjoy life more, our wives enjoy us more. This sort of relaxation shouldn't require a week in the Caribbean. Take stock of your life. Are you enjoying your day-to-day existence? If you were spending a day with a clone of yourself, would you enjoy the company? If not, it may be time to shift your priorities. Sure, there are many things about our lives we're forced to endure for the time being, but what can you do to improve things? Should you change jobs, see your friends more, exercise, pray, or try to leave your work at work? Do what you need to do to be an enjoyable companion.

Forgiveness

Disagreements are inevitable, but our wives said they feel loved when we take the time to forgive.

Our years as psychotherapists have shown that holding a grudge is a deadly thing. When a victim has been wronged, they have all the power—only when they decide to forgive will the playing field be leveled. We've seen couples hold grudges for decades—and their relationship has suffered as a result.

If you and your wife have had disagreements, you need to reconcile, though it's easier said than done. A man once said that his wife momentarily forgot where he went to college, and he has never forgiven her. This was twenty-five years ago. Research has shown that it's the one who forgives who benefits most from forgiveness.[1] The stress of holding on to resentment damages the relationship as well as the physical health of the grudge holder.

So make an effort to forgive any wrong. Talk about the problem; verbalize your hurt and anger; try to understand why the wrong occurred and take steps to prevent it from happening again. Promise your wife that you won't dredge up this conflict to use as ammunition in a future argument. Your relationship health, as well as your physical health, may depend on it.

Lovemaking

You didn't think we'd forget this, did you? The physical act of lovemaking is incredibly important to our wives. Our actions, promises, and words can communicate our love for our wives, but these avenues are not always sufficient. The act of lovemaking—the primal, physical connection and release—conveys our potent love for one another. One night of passionate lovemaking—when you are truly *with* your wife—is worth a million words or thoughtful acts.

Make your love life a priority. Schedule it, surprise her, or together plan an evening alone—just make it happen.

The F.R.E.E. Way to Love Your Wife

Just as God showed his love by sending Jesus to be "God *with* us," loving your wife means that you prioritize your time and energy to be *with* her. You don't have to handcuff yourself to her, but make the time to know her and continuously invite her into relationship with you. Don't take our word for it. Ask your wife how she feels most loved by you.

We have summed up the information in this chapter in a simple formula—the F.R.E.E. way to love your wife:

Focus: Create a sexual mission statement (see chapter 12), reflect on your wedding vows, and meditate on 1 Corinthians 13. Be aware of your strengths and your areas that need growth. Make your relationship a top priority.

Respect: Learn your wife's needs, wants, and desires. Be aware of her insecurities and areas where growth is needed. Trust her with your vulnerabilities and limitations.

Empathize: Listen to your wife. Try to see the world through her eyes. Be mindful of her feelings, and sacrifice your own needs for hers when possible.

Engage: Work to be with your wife during conversations and lovemaking. Forget about work and make efforts to communicate, resolve conflicts, and make love with her whenever possible.

9

Knowing How to Make Love

You didn't skip ahead to this chapter, did you? We would have been tempted to! If you did, go back and read the rest of the book. What you learn here won't work if you haven't mastered the other parts of being a man in relationship with a woman. Though your wife wants you to know about sexual technique, you need to know more about sustaining a great marriage if you want to have great sex.

Sexual technique is a bit overrated. You've probably heard stories about two people who, after having just met, had earth-shattering sex. They might have attributed this to chemistry or sexual prowess—they thought they had great sex because there was something about the other person that made his or her sexual performance extraordinary. That may make a good episode of *Desperate Housewives* or *Sex in the City*, but it's not reality.

Allow us to introduce a piece of psychobabble jargon known as "projection." Projection occurs when we make someone the embodiment of our fantasies or fears. The person becomes a blank movie screen and you're a movie projector. You project onto the screen what you want to see. This happens when we meet someone for the first time. We have hopes, fears, and preconceived notions that we ascribe to the person without verification. We all do it, and recognizing this tendency is the best most of us can do.

When two people who aren't in a long-term relationship have "great sex," it's because of projection. They have the luxury of being divorced from reality. They can imagine the other as a perfect, extraordinary lover. It has little to do with the real person. It's on the same continuum as pornography—if a woman isn't "real," she can meet all of your needs without frustrating, boring, irritating, or intimidating you. Our powerful projections trick us into thinking that we get exactly what we want.

Projection doesn't work as well in a marriage. Actually it does, but people are more likely to project fear and anger onto their spouse after a few years of marriage. The kind of projection that makes for fantasy sex, however, is harder to conjure. If you used to have amazing sex with your wife but now find things lackluster in the bedroom, it's not because one of you is "bad" at making love; it's because your fantasies don't work anymore. You know each other now. You've gotten in fights. You've smelled each other's farts. You've both experienced the other when he or she was anything but sexy.

That's the reason great sex is a lifestyle. Learning some new moves won't help unless you've nurtured a healthy relationship, making the reality of your marriage as good as it can be instead of relying on the fantasies that excited you early on.

The sexual techniques we discuss in this chapter are reality based. We're not going to create a fantasy environment and facilitate projections so you can have great sex temporarily. Getting away for a romantic weekend is wonderful and important, but we're going to talk about how to have great sex after work on a Tuesday. You want to be a great lover in reality, not just in fantasy. If your being a great lover requires a view of white beaches from the balcony of your suite while you sip strawberry daiquiris, you won't have a lot of great sex unless you live in Kauai.

We're going to suggest a program for great sex anytime, anywhere (except in public). You'll find an evening of amazing lovemaking outlined below, but these are suggestions rather than rules or guidelines. Everyone is different, so you'll have to fine-tune things to fit you and your wife. Experiment if you're uncertain. Have fun and try new things until you develop your own unique formula for a night of spectacular sex.

A final thing before we get to the main event: don't expect the formula to work every time. This will be especially true when your wife is upset with you, one of you isn't feeling well, or your relationship is in a tough place. Great lovers are marathoners not sprinters. Your goal should be to improve your sex life over time. Because there are no magic tricks for great sex whenever you want it, you'll need to work at it. However, we'll look at the ingredients many men have used successfully to cook up a hot and spicy night with their wife. Sometimes things won't come together, but when they do . . . well, you'll see.

Ten Steps to an Evening of Great Sex

The following ten steps are *suggestions* not rules. You don't have to complete all ten steps in order (this is not like a manual for building a workbench), and you'll want to be sure to check them out with your wife or even schedule an evening with her to try them. Don't plan on executing this program without your wife's agreement. None of these ideas replaces communicating with her and knowing her desires.

If you aren't emotionally present with your wife, none of these tips will help. (Don't let your wife catch you reading this book under the covers with a flashlight during sex.) Your top priority is creating intense intimacy with her. That can't be scripted, and it's not something you do by rote. Focus on your wife and the love you feel for her rather than the specifics of sexual performance. As long as you do that, you can botch every step below and still have an amazing experience.

A word of warning: we aren't going to be shy with terms and specifics. If our detailed descriptions don't surprise you, some of our language may. We don't use profanity or degrading words, but we employ some slang and euphemisms for sexual terms. Let's be honest. We all hate using words like *penis* and *testicles*, especially when we have heard much more colorful terms in the locker room. We're going to employ words and euphemisms that are fun and sexy—many of the ones we learned earlier that come straight from the Bible (see chapter 1).

Now on to seducing your wife.

Step 1: Clean the House

A few months after one of our clients got married, he did something unusual. He cleaned the house. His wife returned home to find him scrubbing the kitchen floor. He hadn't showered or shaved and looked and smelled pretty foul. Imagine his surprise when his wife said, "Keep this up and you're gonna get some later."

When he looked at his wife with a mix of delight and confusion, she just laughed. But he started scrubbing harder. That night his wife was true to her word—and how.

The man had an epiphany. Cleaning the house turned his wife on. This was shocking because nowhere in his mind was there a connection between mopping the floor and having sex (unless, perhaps, one were to mop naked). His wife, however, saw it as an act of love. It turned her on that he would be considerate enough to do something that he didn't enjoy just to make her happy.

If you want to lay the groundwork for getting laid, do some work for your wife. Cleaning the house seems to work for most guys, but do whatever you know your wife will appreciate most at the moment. If she's been dreading giving the dog a bath, turn the hose on Fido. If picking up the kids from school takes up a lot of her day, cut out of work early and do it for her. It doesn't have to be something that takes all day, but you should be going out of your way to do something your wife will appreciate.

Oh, and if for some reason she doesn't notice that the dog is now spotless and smells like gardenias, don't hesitate to tell her. You should have a servant's heart about whatever you do, but it's okay to help her notice.

Step 2: Clean Yourself

Most women don't like sex with a man who's dirty or stinky, so take a quick shower, and brush your teeth. Go crazy and put on some cologne she likes, but don't drown yourself in the stuff. You might also want to shave again. It will help if your cheek doesn't feel like sandpaper on her cheek ... or her thigh. (Settle down, tiger. We'll get to that in a minute.)

Step 3: Listen

This is the step that men probably miss the most often, because we don't understand its importance. When it comes to romance, we pretty much want to skip straight to the bone dance. Having someone listen to us about all the minor victories, defeats, and oddities of our day seems inconsequential. For many women, however, it's a crucial part of relating. In general, men talk and listen to impart information or to make each other laugh.[1] Women also talk to exchange information and laugh, but, *in addition*, they use conversation to connect with another person. It's a form of intimacy. Once you understand this, you'll see how listening to your wife and devoting attention to the specifics of her day will make her feel closer to you. So ask about her friends, her family, her work, and anything else that's important to her. You'll make her feel special, you'll discover more about her, and the two of you will feel more intimate—and feeling more intimate increases the odds for hot sex.

Step 4: Romance

Now it's time to move things in the direction of foreplay. After some attentive conversation, do something romantic. This can be anything from a small gesture to an extravagant night out. It's different, however, from cleaning the house, which expresses affection indirectly. Now you're going to do something explicit and direct. It may be giving her flowers, cooking her dinner, bringing her a cup of coffee, opening a bottle of her favorite wine, giving her a foot massage, or enjoying a romantic movie together. Romantic dates are great, but a small, unexpected gesture on a busy weeknight can be just as effective.

Regardless of what you do, verbal affection should accompany the gesture. Don't just toss a bouquet at your wife and say, "Ready to shag?" Tell her that you love her. Tell her something you love about her, something you don't express often enough. Then give her a hug. Make her feel special, beautiful, and loved.

Step 5: Foreplay, Part 1

If the first four steps have gone well, it's time to move things toward the bedroom. By this point, your wife should have an idea of what you're up to. If not, she's about to figure it out.

Begin to initiate physical intimacy. Start with something that isn't overtly sexual. In other words, don't start by grabbing her boobs. Give her a massage. Caress her hands or stroke her hair. Cuddle with her on the couch while listening to mood music. Provide the kind of physical affection your wife enjoys. It should be something that doesn't involve direct sexual stimulation but something pleasant and relaxing. Finish this first round of foreplay by giving your wife a gentle but passionate kiss (no tongue yet unless she jumps the gun and swallows you whole). Then ask her if she wants to go to the bedroom (unless you're already there or in a place where you both enjoy having sex).

Take plenty of time with physical affection that's not directly sexual. It will set a mood and build up your wife's desire. Think of her as a volcano—it may take a long time to build up enough pressure for an eruption, but when one occurs, it's powerful enough to wipe out an entire ecosystem.

Step 6: Foreplay, Part 2

If this book were a movie, steps six through nine would warrant an R rating, maybe even NC-17. You've been warned.

Here's a general rule for everything we're about to discuss. Remember this alone and you'll become a master at physical foreplay: *soft to firm, slow to fast. Repeat.* Make this your mantra when touching your wife, and soon she'll be asking you to "come look at something in the bedroom" at every opportunity.

Don't rush foreplay. As we learned from the Song of Songs, anticipation is the best part. The more foreplay, the better the sex will be. You're trying to work your wife and yourself into a lather of sexual arousal. The more time you devote to foreplay, the better the sex will be for both of you. Yes, *both* of you. The male orgasm varies in intensity, just as the female's does. If you take more time for your own sexual arousal, you'll prolong sexual pleasure and your orgasm will feel much better than if you had a "quickie." You're a bit of a volcano yourself.

Start with hugging and kissing. Make an effort to be creative and passionate. Part of the problem with kissing is that it becomes reflexive. We stop thinking about how to give a good kiss. One of the biggest mistakes men make with their wives during sex is not kissing them enough. Instead of just plunging in, imagine that you're kissing your wife for the first time and you want it to be a kiss she remembers. Kiss her face, kiss each of her lips, and caress her tongue with yours. Begin softly, then become more passionate, then slow down and do it again.

Things may start to heat up a little bit. Now you're going to begin focusing on your wife's erogenous zones, the areas of her body that increase sexual desire and arousal when stimulated. Many men think that they have only one erogenous zone—their vine—while their wife has only two—the breasts and vagina. Not true. Several areas of the body, when stimulated properly and at the right time, increase sexual desire and arousal. While guys aren't as responsive to erogenous zones above the waist, women are.

We told you what the erogenous zones are in chapter 4. Now we'll give you some ideas about what to do with them.

LIPS

If you want to drive your wife nuts (in a good way), try this. First, kiss her with passion and creativity as described above. Hug her and let your hands roam around her body a bit. Then move your hands away and focus everything on the kiss. Don't return your hands until she pulls you closer.

EARS

The ears contain clusters of nerve endings, making them sensitive to stimulation. Kiss her ears, caress her ear lobes, and blow into her ear. By the way, that last part isn't done by blowing into her ear like you would blow out a candle. Put your mouth over her ear, breathe into it slowly, and caress her ear with your tongue.

HAIR

Play with her hair, massage her scalp, and run your fingers through her hair. Just make sure not to pull her hair or scratch her head as you would your dog. Be slow and gentle. Try running the tips of your fingers across her scalp as you kiss her face all over.

NECK

The neck is a failsafe female erogenous zone. A great way to initiate sex is to give your wife a back and neck massage and begin kissing her neck. Start with light kisses on the back of her neck. Then work around toward the front of her neck as your kisses become firm and faster. Do this until your wife seems sufficiently aroused, then move down her neck to her . . .

BREASTS

Thought we'd never get here, didn't you? It's important to work your way down gradually to "second base" instead of copping a feel the moment foreplay begins. A woman's breasts are sensitive. If she's not sufficiently aroused, touching or kissing her breasts may tickle or make her uncomfortable. Spend plenty of time kissing and caressing other areas before you kiss her breasts.

Most guys overdo it on the fawns, so you're going to take a different approach. First, start with light, brief touches with your hand, then use your mouth. Don't linger at first. Caress or kiss the breasts, move to another part of her body, then return. Each time you return, spend a little longer time there before you move away.

When you do begin to focus on her clusters, remember your mantra: *soft to firm, slow to fast*. With the boobs we're going to add *outside to inside*. Begin by caressing then kissing the outer area of her breasts. Using your fingers or tongue, draw concentric circles that begin on the outside of her breast and work in toward the nipple. The nipple and areola (the dark circle around the nipple) are extremely sensitive. You should know from your wife's reaction when she's ready for you to spend more time there. Even then, don't neglect other areas of the breast and don't focus on one breast to the exclusion of the other. Give both fawns equal attention. Work up and down the palm before you come back to the clusters. Also give some attention to the often forgotten underside of the breast, which is more sensitive than most men realize.

All breasts, regardless of size, have the same number of nerve endings. This means that small breasts have nerve endings clustered close together. As a result, a woman with small breasts is more sensitive and will likely be aroused more quickly by breast stimulation. The nerve endings will be more spread out on larger breasts, meaning it will take more time. But don't be discouraged if your wife is well endowed. She can be aroused by kisses and caresses on her breasts; it will just take more time and sometimes more intensity (for example, sucking instead of kissing). I doubt you'll mind.

By the time your wife is ready for *firm and fast* around her nipples, adjust the intensity according to what she likes. Some women prefer soft kisses, while some women like hard sucking or even biting. Some women love it when the nipple gets stimulated with just the tip of their husband's tongue, much the way he'd stimulate her clitoris during oral sex. Ask your wife what she likes or observe her reaction. Then give her what she wants.

BACK

After you're well into foreplay, have your wife take off her shirt, unsnap her bra, and roll onto her stomach. Get some lotion that she likes, put some on your hands, and rub your hands together vigorously to warm up the lotion (though letting a cold drop hit her back as a tease can be fun—if it doesn't get you killed). Then massage the lotion into her back. After that, start kissing her neck and back, covering all the way from the lower back up to her neck. The small of her back is particularly sensitive and a good place to visit before the main event. Just make sure you've rubbed the lotion in thoroughly, unless you like the taste.

THE REST OF THE SKIN

The skin is the largest organ of the body, and it's filled with nerve endings that vary in concentration in different areas. Have fun exploring the whole body to discover what turns your wife on. Caress and kiss her legs, buttocks, feet, arms, hands, fingers, and everywhere else. Yes, *everywhere*. Christians can be kinky too, and that place you think your wife would never let you touch or kiss may be just the place that turns her on. Be sensitive; talk to her and gauge her response, but be willing to take some risks. Passion and vulnerability go hand in hand, and you'll both need to be open to new things if you want to have the best lovemaking possible.

YOUR BODY

Be open to different erogenous zones on your body as well. Many of them will be similar to those of your wife, but some will be different. Most guys think of foreplay as going through the motions until the stag gets released into the garden. Calm down, breathe deeply, close your eyes, and enjoy the full experience instead of chugging ahead like a freight train bound for an ejaculation. Let your wife explore your body. Trust your wife as she trusts you. Relax and be patient. Your orgasm is on the way, but it won't be as good if you rush it and miss some cool sensations along the way.

Step 7: Genital Stimulation

And now the moment you've been waiting for.

It's okay to skip this step and move directly to sexual intercourse, but genital stimulation beforehand will prolong and intensify the experience. Also, some women can't achieve orgasm through intercourse, so you may have to stimulate your wife's clitoris another way. In fact, it's possible to have amazing sex even if the stag never enters the garden.

One way to stimulate each other's genitals is what's been referred to as "dry humping"—basically, one of you lying on top of the other and rubbing your genitals together. That's just fine, but there are other ways: manually (with your hands) and orally. There are some slight differences between the two, but the technique is the same. And your mantra—*soft to firm, slow to fast*—applies now more than ever.

Your goal is to stimulate your wife's clitoris. It's a tiny knob of pink flesh behind the top of her inner vaginal lips. The clitoris is sensitive and complicated. Different women enjoy different types and amounts of stimulation. For example, some women enjoy direct stimulation with the finger or tongue or through sucking, while others would writhe away in pain. Also, what might feel like too much to your wife at first may be what she prefers after she's aroused and lubricated (wet).

Start by stimulating the clitoris indirectly at first, for example by *gently* and *slowly* massaging the labia. Then, if your wife's clitoris isn't too sensitive, move toward direct stimulation of the clitoris, again starting slowly and softly and making the movement firmer and faster as she becomes more aroused. Figure out what your wife prefers by observing your wife's reaction or, better yet, asking her what she likes. If she doesn't know, then you get to experiment.

That's the big picture, but let's get into some specifics. This is the part where the prudish and squeamish may have a hard time. Suck it up and forge ahead, sir. Otherwise we're leaving this stuff to the likes of *Penthouse Letters* and other sex merchants, and we don't want to do that.

CUNNILINGUS

Cunnilingus simply means oral sex for your wife. She could be missing out big time if you don't go down on her. Some women can't achieve orgasm without oral sex, so you should at least give it a shot. If you've put all the advice up to this point into practice, it shouldn't be too awkward.

Begin by kissing her waist and inner thighs, slowly working your way toward her garden. Kiss and caress the outside of the vagina at first. Then place your tongue between your wife's labia. You're going for a "pointy" tongue, using the tip of your tongue to caress her instead of licking her. Caress back and forth, working your way toward the clitoris. You may need to use your finger to find it. Start by making circular motions around the clitoris with your tongue. It's important that you don't do too much of the same thing or use a lot of repetitive motion at the beginning. Make circles, then reverse direction. Then switch to going up and down across the clitoris with the tip of your tongue. As your wife becomes more aroused, you can speed up the motion and make it more intense.

You might also try inserting the tip of your finger into her vagina while stimulating the clitoris with the tip of your tongue. (It might help to use some K-Y Jelly on your finger if you need more lubrication. This is supposed to feel good for her, not uncomfortable.) Place your finger with your fingernail down. Go in about an inch, and then hook your finger up slightly. Feel for a ridged patch just inside at the top of her vagina. This is the fabled G-spot. If she enjoys it, stimulate this area in rhythm with the stimulation you apply to the clitoris.

A final technical suggestion: if orgasm is the goal and your wife takes awhile, don't feel bad if you need a break. Switch to using your hand or caress another part of her body for a while and start again when you're ready. However, this can interrupt the climb to orgasm for some women, so hang in there if she's getting close.

It's important to pay attention to your wife's signals of arousal— breathing, moaning, and so on. Once you do something that makes her react positively, keep doing it. In general, your goal will be a tiny up and down or circular motion on the clitoris with increasing speed and intensity. This sensation might be too intense for her, so notice her reactions. If she doesn't like it, slow down or soften up. On the other hand, if she says some variation of "Oh, yes!" or "That feels sooo good," then you'd darn well better keep it up. Your wife's responses and desires will be unique, so communication and experimentation are key.

If your wife achieves orgasm during cunnilingus, don't think for a second that it means you're finished and that you can't have intercourse. First of all, she'll probably be well lubricated, and intercourse will be more pleasant. Second, your wife may be capable of multiple orgasms, and cunnilingus followed by intercourse may be just what she wants.

FELLATIO

Fellatio is oral sex for you. Ninety percent of all men admit that they want their wife to give them a blow job. Of the remaining ten percent, half have never had one and the other half lie.

Some women enjoy performing fellatio on their husbands. Others don't mind but prefer not to. The rest refuse.

Fellatio isn't necessary for a great sex life, but it doesn't hurt. It's not unusual if your wife doesn't enjoy performing oral sex on you. After all, the results are a bit messier than they are for cunnilingus. So don't pressure your wife or get angry if she's not too eager to go down on you. But that doesn't mean you have to give up the cause either. Below are a few suggestions on how to make fellatio more pleasant for your wife if she's not already enthusiastic.

Don't cum in her mouth. If your wife is hesitant to try fellatio, assure her that you're going to warn her before you cum. She can finish the job with her hand.

Appeal to her sweet tooth. Remember all the references to food in the Song of Songs? Cover your stag with chocolate syrup, caramel, strawberry syrup, maple syrup . . . heck, use raspberry vinaigrette if that's what she wants. If you're in a bind, grab a candy bar and rub it on your vine until it melts, yielding chocolate-covered nuts. It will make the experience much sweeter for both of you.

Think of a number between 68 and 70. Your wife might be more en-thusiastic about fellatio while *you're* giving *her* oral sex. It can feel like a much more mutual, equal experience because you're sharing the same vulnerability. She'll also be more sexually aroused and perhaps less in-hibited. Mutual oral sex may take some practice before you both find a comfortable position, but it's worth the effort. This can be a fun, uniquely intimate experience and deserves a try.

Don't be afraid to tell your wife what you do and don't like. Women aren't the only ones who are sensitive down there. Gently coach your wife on what feels good and what doesn't. Tell her to cover her teeth with her lips. She'll want you to enjoy it, and she certainly doesn't want to hurt you.

By the way, we're still in the *foreplay* section.

Step 8: Intercourse

Manual stimulation and oral sex can end up being the main event for the evening. Some couples prefer taking turns bringing each other to orgasm orally instead of through intercourse. Though finishing up with oral sex is fine, it's best as a prelude to sexual intercourse.

In the simplest terms, intercourse (also known as coitus) involves in-serting your penis into your wife's vagina. The overall experience should be much more powerful than a mere act of penetration and release. Jesus's metaphor of a man and wife becoming "one flesh" (Matt. 19:5) is realized when the stag enters the garden gate. You are literally inside of her, glued together, moving as one. It's the emotional, spiritual, and physical pinnacle of lovemaking. A union so powerful occurs that only the lifelong commitment of marriage can contain it. When your vine flourishes in her garden, it's an intense, potent, and sacred thing. And it feels incredible.

Some think that intercourse is only "good" if it results in orgasm. Hogwash. One of the biggest obstacles to great sex is an overemphasis on orgasm. If one or both of you feel pressured to produce an orgasm, it makes sex laborious. Suddenly you're involved in something more akin to passing a test than intimacy and sexual pleasure.

Whenever we counsel men or couples experiencing sexual problems, the first thing we tell them is to forget about orgasms for a while. Sex is chock full of pleasure before the point of orgasm. At no time is this truer than during sexual intercourse. To be a great lover during intercourse, you must first abandon orgasm as the primary goal. Think of it as a bonus. We're not trying to "desexualize" the experience—it should still feel amazing and sexy—but we're trying to bring it back to reality. If you pay attention to secular notions of sex, you'd think that orgasm is the only reason to have sex at all. But the real goal is enjoying the deep, close union with your wife. It will feel good physically and provide intimacy like nothing else does.

Because of this, you want the experience to last awhile. You want to enjoy slow, passionate sex with your wife. The only "technical" aspect you need be concerned about is premature ejaculation or erectile dysfunction (impotence). These problems are common and easy to fix for most men. Physicians and sex therapists have dozens of ways to help you.

Focus on the intimacy and pleasure that intercourse provides instead of working on fancy tricks to make your wife scream her head off in ecstasy. As long as you aren't overly focused on orgasm, the sex will be great. Of course, the irony is that this will make sex better and you'll both be more likely to cum.

To demystify intercourse, however, we'll go over some basics to reduce any anxiety and make intercourse more easy and satisfying.

Penetration

Entering your wife's vagina is more complicated than the guys in the locker room made it sound. For starters, it's not like your stag is a guided missile and the vagina is an easy target. Having sex in the dark makes it harder. If you're having trouble, ask your wife to guide you in. It's much better than fumbling around or hitting the wrong target. And a warning to newlyweds—penetration may be painful for your wife. If you're new to sexual activity, enter slowly and gently. The walls of the garden will expand as sexual activity increases, but take things easy at first.

Whether you are newly married or not, don't hesitate to use lubrication, like K-Y Jelly. It may make sex more comfortable for her, and you'll dig the sensation.

Oh, and don't surprise her. You don't have to wait for an engraved invitation, but she should know that you're about to stick it in. Surprising her could end up being a painful experience for both of you.

When it comes to movement during intercourse, remember your motto—*soft to firm, slow to fast.* This applies to the rhythm of your body during intercourse. You'll begin by moving back and forth gently and slowly. Thrust faster and harder in response to the rhythms of your wife's movements. Over time, the two of you can learn to move together at a pace you both enjoy.

Positions

There are about a thousand different sexual positions, and you should try as many as possible. Abandon the ones you don't like, while rotating the ones that you do. A vibrant sex life includes variety, so switch things around. Here are three of the most popular:

The missionary position. This is the traditionalist's favorite and the only motivation you need for doing lower back exercises. The strength, stamina, and flexibility of your lower back is key to prolonging the experience and establishing a pleasurable, rhythmic motion. You can control the movement of your pelvis more if you raise yourself up on your arms, though you may prefer the sensation of being chest to chest. Your wife might try wrapping her legs around yours, to give her more control. Experiment with holding her legs in different positions. Despite its stodgy reputation, there are a lot of variations on the missionary position, especially if your wife is flexible and your lower back is strong—another reason to give yoga a try.

In all the sexual positions we discuss, you can try stimulating the clitoris with your hand. In the missionary position, this involves reaching down past your stomach and caressing your wife's clitoris (or the area near it if the clitoris is too sensitive). Remember, however, that intercourse isn't just about orgasm. Relax and enjoy the sensation of being inside your wife before focusing on anything else.

Your wife on top. Some women enjoy this position more than the previous one, especially if her husband is a big hunk o' man. It also gives her more control over the movement of your stag inside her garden, though don't think that gets you out of doing any work. Again, a strong lower back will enhance control of your pelvis. It's a bit easier for you to stimulate her clitoris with your hand from this position, and with her on top, you'll appreciate the view. Both of you can enjoy the fact that your hands are free.

Having sex with your wife on top also shows her that sex isn't about dominance. When she's on top, she has more control and freedom. This is an excellent position to empower your wife as an equal during sex.

Entering from behind. Yes, doggy style. If you haven't tried this, you're missing out. This position provides a lot of control for both you and your wife, while leaving your hands free to caress her boobs and stimulate her clitoris. She'll be able to rock back and forth with more ease and control. What's more, your nuts rub against her clitoris from this position. You can have incredible sex from behind your wife. If you're feeling a little wild, do it near a mirror so you can see each other's face.

The only tricky part is the initial entry. Make sure she guides you in on this one. Poke her in the wrong place, and things could go south really fast.

These are only three of the most popular positions. You're limited only by your creativity and flexibility. Share your sexual fantasies with each other and let your imaginations run wild. If you're eager to experiment, grab a copy of the *Karma Sutra* and have fun. But remember, this isn't about earning a medal in gymnastics. Variety promotes a healthy sex life, but it's not the most important part. Regardless of positions and orgasms, God created intercourse as the ultimate in physical intimacy. Make that your primary goal, and the rest will be easy.

Step 9: Afterplay

If you want to have great sex for life, you'll give as much attention to what happens *after* sex as you do to foreplay. It lets your wife know that you weren't just getting off. You made love to her, and you want that to continue even though the "sex part" is over.

Plan the afterplay just like you do the foreplay. Have her favorite drink or dessert ready to enjoy. Start a fire or put on some nice music while the two of you cuddle. If it's a busy time or late in the evening, try a few minutes of cuddling or a massage. Or just whisper affectionate words to her while she falls asleep in your arms. The key to afterplay is showing your wife that you want to spend quality time with her after sex.

If you manage to have sex during the day, you can make the afterplay more active. Take her to lunch, a movie, or her favorite museum. Sex doesn't have to come at the end of the date. Start off a romantic evening with a long, slow time of lovemaking and then go out and have fun together. Then come home and have sex again.

Step 10: Repeat

The best lovers make sex a habit. You're probably a busy man who schedules many things: meetings, jobs, golf, time with your kids, and commitments at church. I doubt that your sex life is less important to you than any of the other things you make time for. Schedule sex like you would anything else. In some Jewish traditions, Friday night, the evening of the Sabbath, is reserved for the husband and wife to get it on. You can do something similar. Pick a night of the week where you set aside plenty of time to make love to your wife, from doing the dishes for her all the way to afterplay. Scheduling sex might not sound very erotic or spontaneous, but spontaneity is overrated when it comes to sex. Being "spontaneous" about sex probably means you don't have it very often. If you and your wife set aside time for sex on a regular basis, you'll enjoy it more. You'll have some less-than-spectacular nights now and then, but don't let those deter you. Being a great lover is a lifestyle not an event. If you make it a point to have sex on a regular basis, your marriage and your overall mental, physical, and emotional health will benefit.

Giving and Receiving

You may wonder why this program seems geared toward seducing and pleasing your wife and not vice versa. The reason for that is simple: you have to give if you want to receive. If your wife sees that you are intentional about attending to her needs, she'll want to do the same for you. It may take some time, because most women don't have sex on the brain as often as we do. Eventually she'll want to know what turns you on. Be sure to tell her and don't be shy. Help her develop a program like this for seducing *you*. You don't have to be the tough guy without needs. Tell her what you like and give her a chance to experiment. Be patient with her. Remember that some sexual practices are an acquired taste. Your wife may not be thrilled with blow jobs at first, but after some time and practice she may grow to like them. It's important that you not be too demanding or put pressure on her—that's a good way to deter her from trying new things. If she feels loved and sees that intimacy with her is what you desire most, she'll be motivated to satisfy your needs.

One more thing: don't underestimate the value of a quickie. While intimacy can't survive on a diet of ten-minute sexual interludes, sometimes it's just what you both need. If your life is hectic and stressful, a quickie can go a long way toward maintaining intimacy with your wife. It also feels thrilling and a little naughty to squeeze sex in when you're "not supposed to," such as during a weekend visit to the in-laws, in free time at a church retreat, during the kids' nap time, or on a lunch break.

Sex doesn't always have to be a major production, but it's something you need to be intentional about. The frequency of sex isn't as important as consistency and communication. A great sex life occurs in reality, not in a fantasy world, and great lovers don't need fantasy for great sex. It takes work, in the context of an imperfect life and a real relationship. Devote time, planning, effort, and attention to your sex life, and you're bound to become an amazing lover. Before long, your reality will be better than most people's fantasies. Then Christian men like you will be role models for sexual prowess, instead of the porn stars and impatient playboys.

10

Knowing How
to Make It Last

May you rejoice in the wife of your youth. A loving doe, a
graceful deer—may her breasts satisfy you always, may you
ever be captivated by her love. . . . Why embrace the bosom
of another man's wife?

Proverbs 5:18–20 NIV

Grow old along with me; the best is yet to be.

Robert Browning

"She had on a white blouse, a blue skirt—and legs. Wow! And legs," said
John Rocchio of the first time he saw his wife Emilia in 1922. "So I says
to myself, 'I need to meet that broad.'" At 101 years old, John has now
been married to Emilia for eighty-two years, the longest marriage in the
world today. But there is no doubt that John loved Emilia for more than
her legs. This couple from Rhode Island has kept their love for each other
as strong today as on the day they were wed. What do they know about

marriage that many couples don't? When recently asked for their secret, Emilia patted John on his arm and said, "Making love!"[1]

How would you answer this question about your own love? How do you keep your own love alive and well? Whether you are forty, sixty, or one hundred years old, there are many ways that you can keep making love to your wife. Making love doesn't just happen in the bedroom. It started when you said "I do" to her on your wedding day. But you must keep saying "I do" every day.

I *do* make it a priority to talk and share with her.

I *do* strive to be a man that she can respect.

I *do* show love and respect to her.

I *do* let her know when something is bothering me, so that we can talk it out.

I *do* control my fantasies and temptations for the sake of our marriage.

I *do* and I always will fight against anything that would take away from our love.

To make love forever also means to battle against the forces that would come against your love. Married love is meant to last forever, but half of all marriages end in divorce instead of "till death do us part." Although there are many reasons for divorce, there are several common ones that all men must guard against. Christian men must protect their love just as an offensive linesman is responsible to protect his quarterback. If the linesman doesn't do his job, the quarterback gets sacked. Don't let your marriage get sacked.

The Bible calls these marriage wreckers "foxes." As the young couple in the Song of Songs warned: "Catch us the foxes, the little foxes, that ruin the vineyards—for our vineyards are in blossom" (2:15). Even though they were drunk with rapturous love, they were also on the lookout for the foxes. Foxes are wily, cunning animals, so it requires vigilance to catch them.

Let's go on a foxhunt.

The Fox of "Extraterrestrial" Affairs

Remember how everything looked so perfect on your wedding day? Even if it was raining out, nothing could take away from how perfect your wife looked to you. She took your breath away as she walked down the aisle to your waiting arms. Out of the billions of other women in the world, you chose her alone. No other woman could compare, and you thought you wouldn't notice another woman for the rest of your life.

That's how I (RR) felt on my wedding day—until the next day. As our plane flew across the Pacific for our honeymoon in Kauai, I was the happiest man on planet Earth. Beside me was the most beautiful wife that a man could hope for. She was all that I had ever dreamed of in a woman. Throughout our flight, I couldn't keep my eyes off my new bride. At a stopover in Honolulu, I could hardly wait for our connecting flight to take us to our island of newlywed bliss and nonstop sexual passion. But then I walked into the airport gift shop. And there, to my surprise, were twelve beautiful and bare-breasted Hawaiian women smiling at me—from the calendar rack. In the blink of an eye (several blinks), I had a strange and startling epiphany. Here I was, the most happily married man in the world, and twelve months of naked women had already captured my eye. It wasn't that they were more attractive than my wife—she could have been a model for the calendar herself. So how, so soon after our wedding, could other women sexually arouse me? How could this happen to me?

It happened because I was still a male. Marriage hadn't changed my masculine nature one iota. I didn't want to notice any other woman besides my new bride, but men notice pretty women—whether we have been married for one day or for two decades.

Soon my wife and I will celebrate our twentieth anniversary on Bora Bora. Even before we go, I already know that there will be more than twelve Polynesian women on the beaches there—topless too. We have been to Tahiti before, and it's not just photos of beautiful women in the

South Pacific—you meet them every day. But I don't have the instant shame or disappointment with myself around other women anymore. My bond has grown deeper with my wife since that day in the Honolulu airport, and my respect and appreciation for my masculine sexuality are deeper too. After twenty years I've learned that I can notice other women (I'd have to be blind to say otherwise) and leave it at that. My temptations are a fox that I can capture, not the other way around.

A Christian man will always notice other women, but he can't let the temptation to look with lust have a hold on him. Instead, he must hold on to his love for his wife. This is the Bible's secret for lasting satisfaction in marriage. The wisdom in Proverbs, written more than three thousand years ago, is just as relevant to husbands today: "May you rejoice in the wife of your youth . . . may her breasts satisfy you always, may you ever be captivated by her love. . . . Why embrace the bosom of another man's wife?" (Prov. 5:18–20 NIV). The tenth commandment expresses the same wisdom by telling men not to covet another man's wife. This restriction actually gives a man the freedom for the greatest sex life. The Bible teaches that your greatest sexual satisfaction begins and ends with your wife. This boundary gives men the freedom to be captivated by their wife's love and breasts.

A Christian man can go to Bora Bora with his wife, be surrounded by topless women, and be the happiest man on the beach. Yet he will be even happier when he gets back to his bungalow with his bride. His greatest satisfaction is when he's alone with his wife. This way is far better than feeling like the guiltiest man on the beach—too many Christian men feel nothing but guilt for their sexual attractions to women. It is not a sin to be attracted to other women. It is a sin not to channel your attractions to your wife. Single men also need to practice self-control regarding their attractions. Although unmarried, they can work on developing this virtue now.

Male nature can too easily allow a man to idealize other women, making them seem better than his wife, and these fantasies can often end up in an "extraterrestrial" affair (yes, that was spelled correctly). By idealizing another woman, a man can believe that she is out of this world. He can even believe that she's as perfect as an angel. The truth is, the reason that she can seem like an angel is because you've never lived with her like you have with your wife. Wait till she lives with you for six months, and she won't be an extraterrestrial anymore. She'll be brought down to earth, and she'll bring you down with her.

One husband in therapy said that he needs to stop putting his old girlfriends on a pedestal, because it makes him think less of his wife. I responded that if he had married one of those old girlfriends instead, he could right now be putting his *wife* up on that very same pedestal. He could easily be fantasizing right now about how great life would have been with—his wife. Fantasizing about other women is a lot like looking at a mirage. If the grass always looks greener on the other side, it's simply because it's Astroturf.

The Fox of "I Don't Need to Date My Wife Anymore Now That We're Married"

The fox of "I don't need to date my wife anymore now that we're married" usually sneaks into a marriage by the second year, but especially after the kids come. Other names for this fox can be "taking my wife for granted" or "turning my wife into my mother so why would I want to date her?" This fox leads wives to complain that their husbands acted like Prince Charming when they were boyfriends and then turned into frogs after the wedding.

When we date, we put our best face forward. We shave, behave, and talk for hours. We buy her flowers and take her to surprise places and great restaurants. We may even paint pictures and write songs for her. We'll do the most romantic stuff we can think of. And then, once she likes us enough to marry us, we go into cruise control. But when you cruise, your love will lose. A good way to stop being lazy is to stop thinking of your bride as only your wife. Think of her as your girlfriend, because she still is. Treat her like a girlfriend again. She might even start acting like your girlfriend again. But this time, you'll get to have sex.

The Fox of Fatigue

American husbands are working more than ever and sleeping less than ever. Only one-third of men today get the recommended 8 hours of sleep. Conversely, the average workweek has gone up to 46 hours, and 38 percent of men are working more than 50 hours a week. Nearly 69 percent of happily married couples say that they have problems sleeping. Twelve percent of married adults even sleep alone.

Even if their wife comes to bed wearing a sexy, black see-through chemise, most husbands will still fall asleep. Okay, that's not really true. Most any guy will be wide awake and postpone sleep if he sees his wife like that, but it's true that he won't enjoy his wife as much when he is so tired. And in many cases, he may fall asleep even before she gets into bed. According to a National Sleep Foundation survey in 2001, 52 percent of men said that they spend less time having sex than they did five years ago.[2]

I'm not sure if it is a part of male nature, but it seems to me that men don't like to have a bedtime, even when they're tired. They will stay up late and do anything but get in bed. But remember when you were first married? You couldn't wait to go to bed, and it wasn't to go to sleep. It was "to lie" with your wife in the Old Testament sense. As time passes, many husbands put off going to bed when their wife does. They watch TV or go on the Internet instead. Imagine that. Choosing a television set over sex with your wife. If you are watching TV because your wife refuses to have sex anymore, it's time to talk with her about her feelings. You may need to talk together with a marriage therapist. Yet for most couples, men just need to turn off the TV and turn on to their wives.

We don't need a study to know that sex and a TV in the bedroom don't mix, but surveys prove that it's true. A recent study found that couples with a television in the bedroom have sex half as often as those who don't have a TV there. For men over fifty, the frequency of sexual intercourse with their wives averaged seven times a month without a TV in the bedroom. With television, the frequency dove down to 1.5 times a month.[3] So move the TV out of your bedroom. It's one of the easiest foxes you can get rid of.

Having children also takes a toll on sleep, but it doesn't last forever. Since "love is patient," a Christian man can wait for those good old days to return. Before long, new fathers and mothers will be getting more sleep again, and more sex as well. Having kids is the greatest trade-off in the world for a temporary pause in a man's love life. There is a season for everything in life—time to have sex and time to have babies. The time for sex will return again someday.

The Fox of Bitterness and Anger

Just as wives can see their husbands turn from a prince into a frog after marriage, husbands can play a similar mind game on their wives. Amazingly, we can turn our wife from a beautiful princess into a conniving witch. When you find yourself carrying more feelings of anger than of love for your wife, it's time to go foxhunting again. This isn't a witch hunt. This is a foxhunt for our own bitterness. As the apostle Paul himself bluntly warns us in the Bible, "Get rid of all bitterness" (Eph. 4:3).

A typical source of resentment for men comes from feeling "trapped" by a woman. In comparison to his independence as a bachelor, a husband can feel like he's forever stuck at home. He complains that his wife won't let him go anywhere or do anything. But if you feel trapped, the problem isn't with your wife. It's you. You may be acting like a good boy who is still trying to please his mommy.

In marital counseling sessions, when the husband complains about his wife's possessiveness, the wife will often say, "I didn't know you felt like that!" She didn't know because he never expressed himself to her.

Stop expecting your wife to read your mind. Instead of being free from having a wife, you need to be free to have a life. If she doesn't like to go rock climbing with you, don't resent her for it. Just go and do it with some other friends, and then come back home and make love to her all night. You'll both be happier.

The Fox of Workaholism

Whenever we hear that a cabinet member or senior-level advisor to the president has decided to step down to spend more time with his wife and family, we have a strange reaction. Our first response is, "How could you leave such an exciting and high-profile career? You are trading the White House for your family's house? Are you crazy?" But another part of us has nothing but respect for the guy's resignation. He typically works a hundred hours a week and sees his family only a few times a month.

If faced with such a choice, what would you choose? Where do you lean when it comes to time for your career and time to enjoy your wife and kids? Men often think that financial success is what matters most in life, and they believe their wife thinks so too. There is nothing wrong with a husband who takes pride in providing for his wife and family, but here is the fox: we can spend so much time working that we don't have any time left for our family.

Dave was a computer programmer who came to therapy because his wife was on the verge of leaving him. When asked how many hours he worked, he said 100 hours a week—for the past two years. While his answer was surprising, his wife's resentment wasn't. After two years of a marriage without a husband, she had contacted a lawyer for a divorce.

If you grew up with a very poor father or an abusive and demeaning father, you may be working to please or outshine him. One of the biggest reasons boxing great Oscar De La Hoya fought so hard was to please his demanding father. It was his way of earning his dad's love. If you are working so hard to prove that you are lovable or worthy of respect, stop the clock. Face the hurts or anger from your past and be freed from them. Find a new pace for your work in your life.

Remember that you are married to your wife, not your job. If you wonder what her expectations for your career success are, ask her. Most women care a lot more about spending time with their husband than about spending money. It's difficult to keep a balance between work and wife, but let the balance tip toward your wife.

Making Your Love Last

After eighty-two years of passionate marriage, Emilia Rocchio gives some pragmatic advice for a very long love: "Never wish for the impossible."[4] Her wish for a loving and committed husband was grounded in reality. This wish is possible for men to fulfill. Keep the above foxes out of your marriage, and you'll enjoy the wife of your youth again for the rest of your life.

Your passion for your wife doesn't have to dim with age. Fires that have turned into hot coals can be stirred up into a fire again. Even as your hormones cool, you can still enjoy passionate love. May your heart never learn to give up on love as you fan the smoldering memories of your girlfriend into never-ending passion for your wife. If you keep the foxes out of the vineyard, your soul will always yearn for her. If it's possible for John Rocchio, then it's possible for you.

11

. . . It's *Who* You Know

"Who told you that you were naked?"

Genesis 3:11 NIV

No one knows how God sounded when he asked Adam and Eve this question. Some might imagine an angry, booming voice from the sky accompanied by thunder and lightning. After years of studying the relationship of sexuality and faith, we have concluded that God did not sound angry; we think he sounded sad. We believe God let out a sigh, shook his head, and thought, *They spoiled one of my best gifts. They're self-conscious about their bodies now. They'll cover their genitals and hide their sexuality. Something I created for intimacy and pleasure will become a source of shame and sin. What they should have felt free and joyful about, they will now keep secret. And secrets cause trouble.*

Who told you that you were naked?

It wasn't God. Making you self-conscious about your sexual nature was the last thing on his mind at creation. But ever since the fall, we have lived under a curse. Our fallen nature, our choice of sin instead of faithfulness, has corrupted one of God's greatest gifts. Our distance from God transforms something miraculous, holy, and exciting into something that troubles us. Our sex drive fills our mind with lustful thoughts and sends us scrambling to regain control. We talk about sex only with our closest friends, if at all. We are not proud of this gift, this wonder of God's creation. When we walked away from God at creation, sex became obscene. It became a curse.

Who told you that you were naked?

Maybe it was the Puritans who told you first. Perhaps when you were still a toddler and marveled at your sexuality, your maleness, an adult reprimanded you. You learned very early not to rejoice in your sexuality. You learned to cover it and regard it with fear. When it gave you pleasure, it also gave you shame. God never wanted that. He had something much better in mind.

Who told you that you were naked?

Or was it the pornographers? Maybe they told you that sexuality was good only for selfishness. They convinced you that it was a crass bodily function, a primitive desire to be satisfied, something akin to going to the bathroom. There's nothing special or sacred about it, so why deny yourself? Satisfy every urge without hesitation, they say. The pornographers never made you feel proud of your sexuality the way that God intended. They made it something to be indulged in dark, secret places—places where you hide from God.

Who told you that you were naked?

Whoever did, they were living out the curse of original sin. God never wanted us to know. God didn't want us to wear clothes. He didn't want our genitals to be any more embarrassing than our fingers or toes. God wanted us to be open with him about our sexuality, but ever since the fall, there is nothing we hide more diligently from God. We don't pray about it unless we're begging for forgiveness. We don't praise him for it; we don't rejoice with him because of it. In fact, thinking about God in relationship to sex is a turnoff for many people. We want nothing to do with God when we're having sex, because we think he wants nothing to do with us.

When we treat sex as dangerous, dirty, or debased, we submit to a curse. We give in to the fall, resigned to the fact that sex is forever ruined by our sinful nature. Christians aren't supposed to live that way. Galatians 5:1 says, "For freedom Christ has set you free. Stand firm, therefore, and do not submit again to a yoke of slavery." We are no longer slaves to the curse of sexual shame. When we regard our sexual nature as sinful, we're taking on a yoke that Christ died to remove. We're redeemed and spotless before God. Christ came to forgive and call us to a life of freedom rather than bondage to sin. Why do we behave as if our sexuality is exempt from his redeeming grace?

It's time to live out our freedom from the curse. Our sin tainted God's gift of sexuality, but Christ restored it. Now we can rejoice before God about our sexuality. We can embrace our maleness and enjoy sex. We need to stop hiding like Adam and Eve did, thinking that our nakedness will anger God.

True sexual freedom is spiritual. In 2 Corinthians 3:17 Paul says, "Now the Lord is the Spirit, and where the Spirit of the Lord is, there is freedom." It is essential to draw near to God if your sexuality is to become a source of joy instead of shame. Tell God about your sexual struggles and praise him for sexual intimacy and pleasure. Once we're enthusiastic about bringing our sexuality before God and welcoming his freeing Spirit, the Puritans will lose their suffocating hold on us and the wares of the pornographers will seem broken and dull.

When you give your sexuality to God, he frees it from sin and shame. He releases it from bondage and returns to you something potent and pure. This redeemed sex drive is under your control. You can use it for intimacy and pleasure, rather than *it* using *you*. Once you've achieved such freedom, you'll have the best sex in the world. The Spirit will be with you, even if you never think about God during sex. Praying or shouting praises during sex is fine, but God is probably content if you focus on your wife and have a good time. He might even prefer it. It's like a parent saying, "You kids go have fun and stop worrying about me." You can get it on with your wife without an instant of guilt, shame, or inhibition. God rejoices when you get wild and "dirty" with your wife. To God, dirty is holy when it comes from a place of love, strength, and spiritual freedom. Use what you've learned in this book to revel in holy dirtiness.

Becoming a great lover to your wife isn't enough, however, to turn the tide against the Puritans and pornographers. We must talk and act like sex is a gift rather than a curse. That means refusing to emphasize only the negative and sinful aspects of sex. It means teaching your children to be proud of their sexuality rather than afraid of it. When the topic comes up, whether at church, work, school, a party, or the golf course, don't giggle, smirk, or shirk. Let others see your joy over sexuality. I'm not talking about sharing intimate details or giving a play-by-play of your last romp with your wife, but you need not hide your passion. Let others see that you're comfortable with your sexuality. Show them that you delight in being the best lover you can be.

Wives wish their husbands knew many things about sex. However, for Christian women, the most important thing is not *what* their husbands know, it's *Who* they know. Knowing Christ, accepting his love, and striving to love as he did are essential to being a great lover. Adam represents the old model for manhood—a man who is given a great gift, ruins it through selfishness and fear, and gets cast out of paradise. Jesus is the new model for manhood. He was the greatest Lover to walk the earth. Jesus wasn't ashamed of who he was, and he loved those around him. His love for others was pure, not selfish or insecure. He didn't serve others to meet his own agenda or because he felt guilty or incomplete. He loved others out of his strength because it gave him pleasure. That's the definition of a great lover. Live this way and you'll become more like Jesus, the world's greatest Lover.

PART FOUR

Knowing
and Growing

12

Your Sexual Mission

Men don't want a lecture on how to use power tools; they want hands-on training. We've reached the point where you get to start using your power tools. It's time to evaluate your strengths and weaknesses, set practical goals, and formulate a sexual mission statement.

Where Am I? Evaluating Strengths and Weaknesses

First, it's important to know where you are now—your strengths and weaknesses when it comes to sex. In responding to the following statements, be completely honest. Your answers will help you set the right goals later.

Pop Quiz 1—You

I know how often I want to have sex.	yes	no
I know what my favorite position is.	yes	no
I know what turns me on.	yes	no
I know what time of day I'm most in the mood.	yes	no
I know what makes me feel powerful and excited.	yes	no

I know what makes me feel powerless and disinterested.	yes	no
I know that God is part of my sexuality.	yes	no
I know how to please my wife.	yes	no
I know how important sex is to me.	yes	no
I am comfortable talking about these issues with her.	yes	no

Pop Quiz 2—Her

I know how often she wants to have sex.	yes	no
I know what her favorite position is.	yes	no
I know what turns her on.	yes	no
I know what time of day she's most in the mood.	yes	no
I know what makes her feel romantic.	yes	no
I know what makes her feel disinterested.	yes	no
I know that God is part of her sexuality.	yes	no
I have told my wife what pleases me.	yes	no
I know how important sex is to her.	yes	no
She is comfortable talking about these issues with me.	yes	no

Pop Quiz 3—The Relationship

We regularly discuss our sex life.	yes	no
We talk about our sexual likes and dislikes.	yes	no
We talk about our sexual fantasies.	yes	no
We know each other's sexual history and upbringing.	yes	no
We make our sex life a priority.	yes	no
Sex is not a weapon or a crutch for us.	yes	no
We tell one another when we're not in the mood.	yes	no
We pray about our sex life.	yes	no
We feel free to ask for things in the bedroom.	yes	no
Our sex life is fun and exciting.	yes	no

If you've answered yes to everything, you're either in denial or a sexual dynamo. Your yes answers are your strengths. Enjoy them, as I'm sure your wife does.

As you look over your yes answers, you may see common themes. Perhaps you excel at communication, or you regularly bring God into the relationship. Or maybe you have a strong knowledge of your partner's sexuality, if not your own. Take a moment and jot down your thoughts below regarding your strengths.

Sexual Strengths

_____

_____

_____

_____

_____

Now look at the no answers. Don't panic. None of these problems is set in stone. These are your areas for growth. You're learning the tools to help you overcome each of these areas that need work. So look at the no answers, look for themes, and take a minute to write down your thoughts regarding the areas that need growth. You should identify an area for growth under each of the categories of evaluation: you, her, and your relationship.

Sexual Areas for Growth

_____

_____

_____

_____

_____

Since this is the chapter where we stop learning about power tools and start using them, here's a challenge for you—make that three challenges:

Challenge 1

Go to your wife, share with her your sexual strengths and areas for growth revealed in the previous quizzes, and ask for her feedback. *You are not looking for solutions yet.* We'll get to those soon enough. The challenge is to talk about strengths and growth areas only, not to fix any problems. Tell her what you think. Ask if she agrees or disagrees, or if she has anything to add. Then move on. If she contributes helpful thoughts to your lists of strengths and growth areas, write them down.

Now that you know where you stand, let's take a crack at goal setting.

Establishing Concrete Goals

Now that you have a clear idea of your strengths and of the areas that need growth, you should establish some concrete goals for your sex life. This will give you long-term vision and short-term motivation. To do this, we need to set some guidelines:

1. *Be positive.* "Master the art of cunnilingus" is a much better goal than "Don't ejaculate prematurely."
2. *Don't set goals that are too high.* For example, don't set a goal of having sex every day if you currently have sex once a year. Goals should seem difficult but not impossible.
3. *Don't set goals too low.* Goals should not be so easy that they take no effort to achieve. Be sure to challenge yourself.

Come up with three goals based on what you wrote under "Sexual Areas for Growth." Decide on a goal for each section of the evaluation: you, her, and the relationship. We suggest you spend some time in prayer, asking God to show you where you need to focus. Write out your goal, including the reason you would like to address it and some practical steps toward reaching it. For example, your goal might be: "Increase communication with my wife about sexual issues." The reason you want to work on this goal could be, "Communication creates intimacy; intimacy creates better sex." One practical step for achieving this goal could be, "Spend at least thirty minutes each week talking with my wife about sex while we give each other foot massages."

If you're not sure what goals to set, consider the following possible areas of focus:

sex and intimacy	sex and creativity	sex as a priority
sex and fun	sexual attitudes	sex and my body
sex and spirituality	sex and my history	

Goal 1:

_____

The reason for this goal:

_____

How will I accomplish this goal?

_____

_____

_____

_____

_____

Goal 2:

_____

The reason for this goal:

_____

How will I accomplish this goal?

_____

_____

_____

_____

_____

Goal 3:

_____

The reason for this goal:

_____

How will I accomplish this goal?

_____

_____

_____

_____

_____

_____

You will need to review your goals weekly and evaluate your progress. Show them to your wife, so that she knows what you are trying to do and can encourage you and participate in achieving them where appropriate. Don't get discouraged if you don't see progress or even if you seem to be moving backward. It takes awhile to change old habits. And remember to pray and ask God to honor your desire to change and to help you do it.

After you meet a goal, take the time to enjoy the satisfaction of having done so. Absorb the rewards and observe the progress you have made. All too often, we achieve a goal and move on to another without giving ourselves the proper pat on the back. Celebrate and share your progress with your wife and move on to the next goal.

Challenge 2

Remember those New Year's Eve resolutions you didn't keep or the list of things to do around the house you never seem to finish? That's not going to happen this time. If you accept this challenge, you will call two or three of your closest buddies and tell them about your goals. You're going to ask them to check up on you every couple of weeks, so they can hold you accountable for pursuing your goals. Ask them if you can hold them accountable for any of their goals. Not only will this help you stay committed to your goals, but you will develop stronger, more meaningful friendships as well.

Crafting Your Sexual Mission Statement

All the work of evaluating your strengths and areas for growth and establishing goals leads us to creating your sexual mission statement. This mission statement will become an important part of your success.

All major institutions have mission statements, because they define a clear, sharp focus for their efforts. Some have said that the Christian mission statement is the Apostles' Creed. Others would say John 3:16 or The Great Commission (Matt. 28:16–20). These statements summarize in a few words all the complex ideas, actions, and goals to which a person or a community aspires.

Many organizations have mission statements that are several pages long, some as long as a book. It's great to be that detailed, but I doubt anybody knows such lengthy statements by heart. We're going to develop a mission statement that is as short, clear, powerful, and direct as possible. In order for it to be useful, we want the statement memorizable, which means no more than a sentence or two.

The formula for your mission statement is simple: vision + action = your mission.

"Vision" is the image of who or what you are creating. It is your ideal self—the masculinity you are in the process of achieving or your ideal situation. Flip back and look again at the goals you set for yourself. Are there themes? Do your goals have to do with intimacy? With expressiveness? With sensitivity? With strength? Keep this in mind as you write your mission statement.

We're going to sidestep the whole procrastination/motivation problem by stating the entire mission in the present tense. Many psychologists talk about the power of self-talk. If we tell ourselves something long enough, we will adapt to that statement.

To craft the vision portion of your mission statement, think about the kind of lover you would like to be or the kind of sexual atmosphere you would like to create in your marriage. Consider starting with one of these phrases:

"I create . . ."

"I am . . ."

"I seek . . ."

"I am becoming . . ."

"I produce . . ."

"I achieve . . ."

If you're still not clear, take a look at the vision portions of the mission statements written in one of our workshops:

"I produce an intimate, passionate marriage . . ."

"I am a strong, compassionate, exciting man . . ."

"I achieve epic sexual prowess . . ."

It's a vision, so it's not true of you now; it's what you want to achieve. State it, however, as though it were already a fact.

When you have a clear idea of your vision, write it here:

_____

_____

_____

The action part of your statement expresses how the vision will be achieved. Begin by simply adding the words *by* or *who* to the end of the vision portion, and complete the sentence.

"I produce an intimate, passionate marriage *by* regularly expressing my deepest needs to my wife."

"I am a strong, compassionate, exciting man *who* seeks contact with God and my wife daily."

"I achieve epic sexual prowess *by* experimenting in the bedroom, working out, being a man among men, and seeking my Lord daily."

Add your action phrase to your vision phrase to create your own mission statement below:

_____

_____

_____

Challenge 3

If we repeat an action daily for twenty-one days, it increases the likelihood that it will become a habit. Also, it is easier to remember to do something each day if it is paired with another task. Therefore, we challenge you to memorize your mission statement and repeat it at the same time each day (for example, while shaving, when you eat lunch, when you flip on ESPN, and so on) for three weeks. This will firmly plant the statement in your mind.

Nice work. You've evaluated yourself, set goals, and created a sexual mission statement. Hopefully, you understand yourself a little better. If you took the challenges, you've also opened up communication with your wife and your friends and made a commitment to your mission statement. That's a lot of work for one day. You deserve to celebrate. Go have sex!

13

What Men Wish
Their Wives Knew

I t is our hope that, though this book was written for men, there will
be many wives who will want to take a look at it. At least, men, you
can let them know that there is a chapter in it for them. We know, wives,
that you are just as curious about sex as men are, and we appreciate your
desire to learn and to grow. We all want our sex lives to melt the paint
off the walls, and, with a little teamwork, you and your husband can
get there. For Christians to have the best sex, men and women need to
work together.

Throughout this book we've told men what they need to know to
make their sexual wishes come true. Now it's your turn to hear what
your husbands wish from you. While men and women are different right
down to their DNA, we are surprisingly similar when it comes to our
need for love. Here are some ways that you can make love to your man
and make his sexual wishes come true.

Trust Him

My wife and I (RH) have a tradition. Once a year, we set aside time for a vacation and I plan it—everything. I don't tell her anything about it. She doesn't know where we're going until we step on to the airplane. Some friends tell her she's nuts for trusting me with precious vacation time, but we both love this tradition because we each get something out of it. She is treated to a nice surprise, and I am reminded of her trust.

It's not always easy for her to trust. I've made less-than-stellar travel plans in the past, and I've forgotten a few important elements (like telling her to pack a jacket for a ski trip) that would justify her distrusting me. But the fact that she does trust me makes me work harder to keep her trust. That's the secret. I know she bites her tongue sometimes, resisting the urge to tell me what to do and how to do it, and for that I feel gratitude, so much gratitude that I put extra effort into being a trustworthy man.

How much do you trust your man? When's the last time you put yourself in his hands? We feel loved when you tell us and show us that you trust us.

There may be times however, when we show ourselves to be untrustworthy. We've let you down, perhaps hurting your feelings and damaging the trust between us in the process. Help us rebuild that trust by (1) letting us know what we've done wrong and how it feels, (2) giving us the opportunity to earn trust through small things, then work up to bigger ones, and (3) trying to think back to good decisions and actions of ours in the past. Open communication, prayer, and a spirit of forgiveness go a long way when it comes to rebuilding trust.

Appreciate His Work and Talents

Most men wish that they could not only provide for their wife and kids but also have plenty of money left over so they could wine and dine their wife forever and buy her whatever she wants. Since work and worth are nearly synonymous for men, the way your husband provides for you can be his greatest source of shame. Although you may think his career and income are adequate, he may think just the opposite. If your man has insecurities concerning how he provides for his family (and most men do), he will be less confident to romance you and get closer to you. He may even avoid you.

A good way to boost your man's self-confidence and closeness with you is to show esteem for his work. Tell him that you appreciate his hard work. Men love to be respected for their work ethic. On the other hand, if you feel your man works too much, let him know that too. Some men need to slow down and spend more time with their wife than with their job. Reassure him that you will still feel secure even if he cuts back at work.

Another way to esteem your man is to respect his talents outside of his work. Men need to invest their talents in pursuits or hobbies as well as their careers. When he does, give him some recognition, even if you're not crazy about his trumpet playing or trout fishing. Other talents may include mentoring kids, teaching Bible studies, fixing things around the house, landscaping, or coaching Little League. If for some reason your husband isn't investing his talents like this, you could encourage him to start. Some husbands might avoid investing in their talents because they fear they won't have your support.

When a man knows that his wife appreciates his work and talents, he will feel greater confidence in himself. That confidence will renew his motivation to take care of your needs—financially, emotionally, and sexually. He will feel sexier in your eyes, and you will look sexier in his. Respect is an amazing aphrodisiac.

Take Pride in Your Own Talents

Jesus used the parable of the talents (Luke 19:11–26) to show how we are rewarded for using the gifts he gave us. This also applies to your marriage. When you share your innate talents and gifts for the good of the marriage, both you and your husband benefit.

Take a minute to review your unique gifts. Are you an entrepreneur, an artist, a prayer warrior, or a great communicator? Do you possess a talent for organization, are you compassionate, or do you have a sense of humor? Husbands feel loved when their wife uses her gifts to enhance their home and their relationship. And when you feel free to use your gifts, so will he.

Be Patient with Him

Men aren't famous for expressing emotions. Sometimes we let pride cloud our judgment, and we can be stubborn. Most of us are works in progress. We need time to grow in these areas, and we need your support.

Some couples sit down together periodically and discuss their goals for themselves as individuals and for their relationship. Think about doing this together, and offer support for each other's goals. You'll find you have a different view on patience when you're working together as a team. It will be easier for him to be patient with you if he feels that you're patient with him.

Communicate with Him

From birth, males don't read emotional cues as well as women. A study at the University of Cambridge observed infants who were only one day old in a newborn nursery. Each baby was shown two different faces. One face was that of a female student leaning over the crib. The other was a mobile picture of the same female that was an abstract mix of her facial features. The girls spent more time looking at the woman; the boys spent more time looking at the object. In a similar study, at one year of age, female and male babies showed a difference in their attention to films.

Girls looked longer at films with faces, while boys preferred watching films with cars! Studies of college women also confirm that women are much better than men at reading both the verbal and nonverbal cues of someone's emotions.[1]

Women's brains are wired for cueing in on emotions. The frontal cortex and the limbic cortex process our higher cognitive and emotional responses, and both are denser in the female brain. Not only do women have a greater capacity to read feelings, they also have a greater capacity to express them.

Our centers of language are found in the frontal and temporal lobes of the brain. Again, these lobes are larger in women's brains than in men's. Further, women process verbal language simultaneously in both sides of their frontal brain, while men tend to process it in the left side only. The corpus callosum, the band of fibers that connects the left and right brains together, is larger in women than in men. This means that when women speak, they access both sides of their brains faster than do men, weighing both logic and their feelings. By the time a man's thoughts get from his logic-oriented left brain into the feeling-oriented right brain, a woman has already been there and back.

Women verbalize their feelings more than men; they are also more intuitive. Some women have a way of knowing what someone thinks or feels without needing to hear the words. Unfortunately, most men aren't so intuitive. Something may be painfully obvious to you, but your man hasn't a clue.

Sometimes we need to be told information in exquisite detail. Maybe you had a bad day and want to talk about it. So you come in the room, throw down your bag, and give a big sigh. Believe it or not, most of us at this point don't know you've had a bad day and want to talk. You then get mad at us for being insensitive, and we tell you that we're not mind readers. Just tell us how you feel and what you want. That includes what you want in bed. You may be shocked to find how willing we are to oblige.

Surprise Him

Men like surprises too. My wife went on a trip recently and left a love note for me to find on my can of antifungal foot spray. It was awesome. Surprises help us know that you spend time thinking about us when we're apart. They're fun too.

Of course, surprises can come in many different forms. It takes really knowing your man to know how to give him a meaningful surprise. If you talk with him long enough about his dreams, goals, and fantasies, good surprise material will emerge.

Have Fun

One of the greatest gifts you can give your husband is enjoying your life together. Whether you realize it or not, men spend a lot of time thinking about their wives' happiness. Most men worry in silence, so you might not know how concerned your husband is when you aren't happy. He also might not sufficiently communicate how good he feels when you are happy. When we see you feeling good, enjoying yourself, laughing, or relaxing, we relax too. We like it when you feel good about yourself, so let us know if we can help.

Forgive Him

If we're going to be dance partners for the rest of our lives, stepping on toes is inevitable. We need forgiveness on a regular basis.

Forgiveness means believing your husband when he says he's sorry. It also means letting go of resentments. After you've been married for thirty-two years, don't bring up to your parents what a jerk he was on your first date. If he makes a sincere apology and changes his behavior, let go of the grudge. Holding on to bitterness takes a dangerous toll on a marriage. We've known wives who were so bitter about their husbands' failures that they shunned all physical and sexual intimacy for years.

Grace and forgiveness offer healing for old wounds and erase old records of wrongs. As the Bible says, "See to it that no one misses the grace of God and that no bitter root grows up to cause trouble and defile many" (Heb. 12:15 NIV). If your husband has apologized for his offense, and you have talked out your hurts, forgive him. Letting go of bitterness is one of the best ways to show your love.

Make Love Like He Knows You Can

We know you. We know there's a part of you that wants to let go in the bedroom and be the free, uninhibited sexual diva you're capable of being. Show your husband that side of you. It'll take trust, patience, communication, surprise, and forgiveness to get there, but it will all be worth it. Having exciting sex is what God wants for you and your husband. Our surveys of Christian men reveal that they wish their wife would initiate sex more often. Tell your husband what he can change to make it easier for you.

Enjoy Your Stag

Have you ever thought that men are like animals? We are. Male sexual nature has more in common with roosters and bucks than with the sexual nature of women. Remember that stag jumping around in the Song of Songs, looking for sex with his beloved? That's your Christian man—a real animal. If you marvel at how often your stag thinks about sex and looks at your clusters, consider what it's like for him. We're not asking for pity here, just for some understanding. The truth is that it isn't easy to be male. We can't tell you how many men have told us that they wish they could turn off or at least turn down their sexual desires. They would like to have a break from always having sex on their mind. One study reveals that 86 percent of Christian men think about sex every day, and 16 percent think about sex every hour.[2] With testosterone levels nearly fifteen times higher than yours, it's not a surprise that men are horny all the time. So when you think of your man as an animal, don't demean him or think of him as a dog or a pig. The Bible calls him a stag, and God made him this way for a reason.

God explains the purpose of the male sexual drive in Genesis 1:28, when he told Adam and Eve to "be fruitful and multiply." The first command in the Bible was to have sex, and the male sex drive has carried out this command for generations. In the second chapter of Genesis, we see the second reason for the male sex drive, for a man to be "united with his wife, and they will become one flesh" (Gen. 2:24 NIV). Sex makes you one flesh and creates the closest physical union. It wasn't good for Adam to be alone, and he represents all men. So when you have sex with your husband, you are dispelling loneliness for him. Your husband's sexual desires are good. After creating Adam, God said that it was "very good." If you feel that your husband's sexuality is mostly bad, try to see what is good about it. Try to see what God sees.

Now let's talk about a more difficult and painful aspect of your man's nature—his eyes for other women. If your husband never notices other attractive women, something is not normal with him. Either he has inhibited sexual desire, or he is so burdened with shame that he doesn't allow himself to be human. Some Christian books claim that a man should never notice another woman besides his wife. That's not realistic for any man. Testosterone stimulates the male brain to notice women. It's OK for a husband to comment that his favorite actress is also very beautiful. While noticing attractive women is not a sin, the Bible teaches men to constantly exercise self-control over these attractions. If he flirts with other women or constantly ogles them, tell him to knock it off and control himself. Don't be afraid to tell him when it hurts your feelings. Although his eyes will get distracted now and then, his *heart* should only be longing for you.

Be a Free, Empowered Woman

Men love women who love being women. Your greatest sex appeal to your husband does not come from how much skin you show him or how often you reach for his vine. The sexiest wives are those who feel confident with their own identity, opinions, dreams, and goals. Don't lose your life or identity in him; grow in your own. Men love their wives to be close to them, but they also love their wives' independence. Women who have confidence and self-esteem are a turn-on for men. Your confidence will also help you enjoy sex with your husband more.

When it comes to lovemaking, the bride in the Song of Songs says, "Let him kiss me with the kisses of his mouth" (1:2 NIV) and goes on to have him kiss her everywhere else. This kind of assertion in lovemaking excites men. The Song gives you freedom to seduce your husband. In fact, in the book of Ruth we read of how Naomi taught Ruth to seduce Boaz to become her future husband, lover, and kinsman redeemer. The Bible encourages women to express and enjoy their feminine sexuality and power with men.

Feeling good about yourself is the sexiest thing you can do for your husband. Express what you want and what you don't want. Feel free to initiate sex when you want that too. Feel free to say no if you're not in the mood, but let your husband know that you look forward to loving him again, sooner rather than later.

As your husband tries to love you with all that he's got, consider how you can love him right back. God meant for Christian women to be great lovers too. Like the beloved in the Song of Songs, enjoy your husband's love and be thankful for your stag.

"May your love with him be more delightful than wine."

Song of Songs 1:2

Notes

Chapter 1 Knowing in the Biblical Sense

1. Dietrich Bonhoeffer, *Letters and Papers from Prison* (New York: Collier, 1953), 100.

2. Michael Cosby, *Sex in the Bible: An Introduction to What the Scriptures Teach Us about Sexuality* (New York: Prentice-Hall, 1984), 55.

3. Marcia Falk, *Song of Songs*, Harper's Bible Commentary (San Francisco: Harper & Row, 1988), 525.

Chapter 2 Knowing the Myths and the Truth

1. James Nelson, *Embodiment: An Approach to Sexuality and Christian Theology* (Minneapolis: Augsburg, 1978), 41.

2. T. C. Burnham and others, "Men in Committed, Romantic Relationships Have Lower Testosterone," *Hormones and Behavior* 44, no. 2 (2003): 119–22.

Chapter 3 Knowing How to Be a Man

1. See M. Schuchardt, "Playboy! The Cultural Victory of Hugh Hefner," *Regeneration Quarterly*, July 1, 2001, 31.

2. Althea Horner, *Psychoanalytic Object Relations Therapy* (Northvale, NJ: Jason Aronson, 1991), 32.

3. Patrick Goldstein, "A Difficult Coming of Age," *Los Angeles Times*, February 27, 2001, F4.

4. Robert Bly, *Iron John* (New York: Addison-Wesley, 1990), 16.

Chapter 5 Knowing the Dangers

1. Edward O. Laumann, Anthony Paik, and Raymond C. Rosen, "Sexual Dysfunction in the United States: Prevalence and Predictors," *Journal of the American Medical Association* 281, no. 6 (February 10, 1999): 537–44.
2. *USA Today*, June 13, 2005, www.usatoday.com.
3. C. Lee and R. Glynn Owens, *The Psychology of Men's Health* (New York: McGraw Hill, 2002).

Chapter 6 Knowing Who You Are

1. John Eldredge, *Wild at Heart* (Nashville: Thomas Nelson, 2001), 149.

Chapter 7 Knowing How to Be Alone

1. T. C. Burnham and others, "Men in Committed, Romantic Relationships Have Lower Testosterone."
2. John McCain, "Torture's Terrible Toll," *Newsweek*, November 21, 2005, www.msnbc.msn.com/id/10019179/site/newsweek.
3. Viktor Frankl, *Man's Search for Meaning: An Introduction to Logotherapy* (New York: Pocket Books, 1959), 172.

Chapter 8 Knowing How to Love Her

1. Kathleen A. Lawler, Jarred W. Younger, Rachel L. Piferi, Rebecca L. Jobe, Kimberley Edmundson, and Warren H. Jones, "The Unique Effects of Forgiveness on Health: An Exploration of Pathways," *Journal of Behavioral Medicine* 28, no. 2 (April 2005): 157–67.

Chapter 9 Knowing How to Make Love

1. Deborah Tannen, *You Just Don't Understand* (New York: HarperCollins, 1990), 4.

Chapter 10 Knowing How to Make It Last

1. Sarah Schweitzer, "82 Years Later, R.I. Couple Still Holding Hands," *Boston Globe*, June 23, 2005, www.boston.com.
2. Paul Recer, "You're Not Alone If You Nod Off on the Job," *The Press-Enterprise*, March 28, 2001, www.pe.com.
3. "Want to Sex Up Your Love Life? Turn Off the TV," *Reuters*, January 18, 2006, www.msnbc.msn.com.
4. Schweitzer, "82 Years Later, R.I. Couple Still Holding Hands."

Chapter 13 What Men Wish Their Wives Knew

1. Larry Cahill, "His Brain, Her Brain," *Scientific American* 295, no. 5 (May 25, 2005), 40–47, www.scientificamerican.com.
2. Archibald Hart, *The Sexual Man: Masculinity without Guilt* (Dallas: Word, 1994), 58–59.

References

Bly, Robert. *Iron John*. New York: Addison-Wesley, 1990.

Bonhoeffer, Dietrich. *Letters and Papers from Prison*. New York: Collier, 1953.

Burnham, T. C., Flynn Chapman, J., Gray, P. B., McIntyre, M. H., Lipson, S. F., and Ellison, P. T. "Men in Committed, Romantic Relationships Have Lower Testosterone." *Hormones and Behavior* 44, no. 2 (2003): 119–22.

Cahill, Larry. "His Brain, Her Brain," *Scientific American* 295, no. 5 (May 25, 2005): 40–47, www.scientificamerican.com.

Cosby, Michael. *Sex in the Bible: An Introduction to What the Scriptures Teach Us about Sexuality*. New York: Prentice-Hall, 1984.

Eldredge, John. *Wild at Heart*. Nashville: Thomas Nelson, 2001.

Falk, Marcia. *Song of Songs*. Harper's Bible Commentary. San Francisco: Harper & Row, 1988.

Frankl, Viktor. *Man's Search for Meaning: An Introduction to Logotherapy*. New York: Pocket Books, 1959.

Hart, Archibald. *The Sexual Man: Masculinity without Guilt*. Dallas: Word, 1994.

Horner, Althea. *Psychoanalytic Object Relations Therapy*. Northvale, NJ: Jason Aronson, 1991.

Lawler, Kathleen A., Younger, Jarred W., Piferi, Rachel L., Jobe, Rebecca L., Edmundson, Kimberley, and Jones, Warren H., "The Unique Effects of Forgiveness on Health: An Exploration of Pathways." *Journal of Behavioral Medicine* 28, no. 2 (April 2005): 157–67.

Laumann, Edward O., Anthony Paik, and Raymond C. Rosen. "Sexual Dysfunction in the United States: Prevalence and Predictors." *Journal of the American Medical Association* 281, no. 6 (February 10, 1999): 537–44.

McCain, John. "Torture's Terrible Toll." *Newsweek*, November 21, 2005, www.msnbc.msn.com/id/10019179/site/newsweek.

Nelson, James. *Embodiment: An Approach to Sexuality and Christian Theology.* Minneapolis: Augsburg, 1978.

Schnarch, David. *Passionate Marriage: Keeping Love and Intimacy Alive in Committed Relationships.* New York: Owl Books, 1997.

Tannen, Deborah. *You Just Don't Understand.* New York: HarperCollins, 1990.

U.S. Senate Judiciary Committee, Subcommittee on Juvenile Justice, 98th Congress, 2nd session (1984). *Effect of Pornography on Women and Children,* 227.

Ryan Howes (PhD, Fuller Theological Seminary) is a clinical psychologist in private practice specializing in men's issues and relationships. He is an adjunct faculty member at Fuller Theological Seminary, Pepperdine University, and Glendale College, where he teaches classes on sexuality and intimate relationships.

Richard Rupp (MDiv, MFT, Fuller Theological Seminary) is a licensed marriage and family therapist in private practice in Pasadena, California, and he has taught at Fuller Theological Seminary. A frequent speaker at men's conferences, Rick has also developed a church-based rite of passage for boys into Christian manhood.

Stephen W. Simpson (PhD, Fuller Theological Seminary) is a psychologist, writer, speaker, and professor at Fuller Theological Seminary.

For private counseling, speaking engagements, or more information about Christian men and sex, visit www.christianmenandsex.com.